Enneagram

Discover Your True Self and Build Relationships

(Real-world Scenarios to Help You Decipher the 9 Personality Types)

James Franck

Published By **Daniel Kaplan**

James Franck

Enneagram: Discover Your True Self and Build Relationships(Real-world Scenarios to Help You Decipher the 9 Personality Types)

ISBN 978-0-9952066-9-4

Legal & Disclaimer

The information contained in this book is not designed to replace or take the place of any form of medicine or professional medical advice. The information in this book has been provided for educational & entertainment purposes only.

The information contained in this book has been compiled from sources deemed reliable, and it is accurate to the best of the Author's knowledge; however, the Author cannot guarantee its accuracy and validity and cannot be held liable for any errors or omissions. Changes are periodically made to this book. You must consult your doctor or get professional medical advice before using any of the suggested remedies, techniques, or information in this book.

Upon using the information contained in this book, you agree to hold harmless the Author from and against any damages, costs, and expenses, including any legal fees potentially resulting from the application of any of the information provided by this guide. This disclaimer applies to any damages or injury caused by the use and application, whether directly or indirectly, of any advice or information presented, whether for breach of contract, tort, negligence, personal injury, criminal intent, or under any other cause of action.

You agree to accept all risks of using the information presented inside this book. You need to consult a professional medical practitioner in order to ensure you are both able and healthy enough to participate in this program.

Table Of Contents

Chapter 1: How Different Enneagram Types Cope

Breakups are difficult, regardless of how lengthy the connection lasts. And they're mainly painful once they appear throughout the Holidays. This is a month complete of satisfaction, activities, affection and gift giving - the entirety that reminds you of your ex and what you've got got out of place.

But bet what? If you're feeling depressed and disturbed, the Enneagram may additionally moreover useful beneficial aid. Your Enneagram type may additionally moreover let you know plenty approximately the way you feel disappointment, making it much less complex as a manner to go through.

Enneagram Type 1 - The Perfectionist

For Type 1s, the Christmas season is big – an outward statement of your beliefs approximately circle of relatives, love and what should be. You have a meticulously constructed photo of a ‘brilliant’ tour, entire with a loving partner by means of the usage of manner of your factor, and could likely commit a whole lot of effort and time in bringing that vision to fact.

The breakup blow:

You exit of your manner to put together a lovable holiday experience; finally it is able to be heartbreaking to have it disrupted with the beneficial resource of a split. The amazing picture you imagined might also moreover function a harsh reflects, reflecting your damaged relationship and what you could view as non-public inferiority. Your inner voice can also slant in the direction of self-blame and condemnation till you intentionally motive in the path of self-compassion.

Coping strategies:

Craft new excursion sporting activities that have been no longer in the unique quality imaginative and prescient to assist separate from your ex.

Do some thing sudden, like last-minute Christmas purchasing, to aid lighten the excessive expectancies you may have.

Practice mindfulness and self-compassion that will help you control the overload.

Enneagram Type 2 - The Giver

The Christmas season is whilst the Type 2's sensitive nature appears the finest. It's a time to have the capacity to expose affection with sports activities like considerate present-giving and emotional help. You experience huge while you may assist make the journey top notch for humans round you.

The breakup blow:

Your loving and giving element comes out in entire pressure throughout the Holidays, so a breakup may additionally rip away a big deliver of your satisfaction and feel of really nicely well worth. You can also moreover experience that you did not meet your ex's desires or that they did no longer appreciate the try you located into making the vacation precise.

Coping techniques:

Provide your self the same love and care you frequently display others. Plan a self-care day entire of your selected Christmas films, meals and relaxation. You deserve it.

Surround your self with appreciative pals and family who reciprocate your giving attitude, making Christmas gatherings a deliver of mutual care and assist.

Enneagram Type three - The Achiever

For Type 3s, the Christmas season is a time to create friendships and characteristic an amazing time the twelve months's triumphs. Whether it's far a merchandising, a modern courting, or a private milestone, the vacations offer you a platform to percent your pleasures with others.

The breakup blow:

At an generation at the identical time as celebrations of personal and social victories are installation, a divorce need to appear to be a public setback for Type 3s. The public detail of Christmas celebrations should exert strain on you to put up a masks of achievement and delight, even within the center of misery.

Coping techniques:

Allow your self to evaluate your emotions and lament the shortage of the connection. It's awesome to now not enjoy all proper, because of the truth that behaving otherwise would likely certainly put off the restoration method.

Focus on what you have were given got executed this 12 months, for my part, define achievement out of doors your romantic conditions.

Foster lasting connections through discussing your sincere sentiments approximately the divorce with honest buddies, perhaps over a non-public dinner or a one-on-one espresso consultation.

Enneagram Type four - The Individualist

For Type 4s, the vacations offer a canvas for displaying your awesome feel of flare, depth, and emotional complexity. You appearance beforehand to the festivities as a time even as the world catches up at the side of your quest for extra significance and large connections.

The breakup blow:

The vacations, a season rich with emotional traditions, also can all of sudden seem tinted with sorrow for Type 4s. The divorce may moreover furthermore trade the Christmas season to a panorama of loss and preference, even as every ceremony seems like a ghost of the beyond.

Coping strategies:

Use your creativity to installation new traditions that replicate the man or woman you are. For example, you can create seasonal décor, personalised presents or elegant vacation cards.

Take a leisurely stroll and reflect. You want time and area to analyze your sentiments. Don't get so stuck up inside the Holidays or nostalgia that you overlook to nurture your internal self.

Enneagram Type 5 - The Investigator

Type 5s spends an entire lot of time studying troubles that spark their hobby, and the Holidays are not any tremendous. Whether it is numerous cultural traditions or the psychology of own family on the dinner desk, you may use this time to pay attention to your precise 'tour venture,' which affords a fascinating and worthwhile hazard a remarkable manner to partake within the celebrations.

The breakup blow:

A breakup provides an extra degree of mirrored picture for Type 5s, who may additionally now overanalyze the connection, striving to recognize what went incorrect. The Holidays are already an emotional high tide for Fives. The expectations of engagement may also additionally want to seem intrusive, an unwelcome distraction to your very own recovery gadget.

Coping strategies:

Set boundaries for yourself. You do no longer need to attend each Christmas celebration or interact in small chat with genuinely everybody. Protect your non-public location and take breaks while you want them.

Use your analytical nature to delve deep into your feelings, allowing yourself to method them in a wholesome manner.

Enneagram Type 6 - The Skeptic

For Type 6s, the Holidays provide stable vicinity in an unpredictable worldwide. Familiar rituals and traditions provide greater than nostalgia – they act as a framework in order to increase your intellectual well-being, answering your name for for stability and predictability.

The breakup blow:

A Christmas breakup disturbs this quiet sanctuary, converting not unusual happiness with uncertainty and scenario. Each Christmas addiction also can now evoke a revel in of loss and project your bear in mind in balance and the destiny.

Coping strategies:

Engage in traditional tour customs that provide warm temperature and decrease anxiety.

Have a well-deliberate holiday schedule with a mix of acquainted activities and useful connections to maintain a revel in of consistency to the season. This also can help reduce your uneasiness.

Leave some room for spontaneity to embrace the vacation spirit, too - often the nicest reminiscences are original inside the surprising times.

Enneagram Type 7 - The Enthusiast

For Type 7s, the Christmas season is associated with pleasure. You're the party planners of the Enneagram. The holidays are an experience-wealthy playground in which you can in fact come alive.

The breakup blow:

The contradiction of grief amid pleasure may be painful for Type 7s. The divide threatens to impair your herbal sensation of delight and journey and, worse, you'll be obliged to deal with your emotions even as you usually avoid terrible feelings in any respect prices.

Chapter 2: Comprehending Enneagram Communication Styles

The Enneagram, consists of nine tremendous man or woman sorts, abilities as a effective method for learning each ourselves and others, specifically in near relationships like marriage. Through recognizing the severa verbal exchange patterns of every kind, we may additionally additionally construct the talents to bridge gaps, conquer troubles, and shape more large relationships.

Below is a test of the numerous verbal exchange styles displayed by way of the usage of the usage of every Enneagram kind:

The Assertive Triad comprised Types eight, 7, and 3.

Type 8 (The Challenger): Direct, effective, and passionate. I strain the attributes of honesty and transparency, and I definitely have a penchant for undertaking open and clean conversations. As a end result, my communique fashion may additionally furthermore from time to time be visible as pushy.

Personality kind 7, called "The Enthusiast," is described with the resource of being glad, exuberant, and brought on through manner of mind. Engage in lively discourse, pass between subjects, and can have problem maintaining popularity at some point of excessive arguments.

The Type 3 personality, additionally known as "The Achiever," is described via the usage of being very goal-orientated, green, and caused thru engaging in goals. Communicate truely, consciousness on solutions, and may be irritated via using prolonged emotional exchanges.

The Feeling Triad (Types 2, 1, and six):

Type 2 (The Helper): Empathetic, annoying, and supportive. They carefully pay interest, fee retaining right relationships, and might hesitate from speakme their very own needs.

Type 1 (The Reformer): Conscientious, principled, and justice-oriented. Value logical reasoning, try for equity, and may be critical or perfectionistic in speakme.

Type 6 (The Loyalist): Security-looking for, collaborative, and detail-oriented. Ask clarifying questions, are seeking out reassurance, and might experience uncomfortable or indecisive in dispute.

The Thinking Triad (Types 5, four, and 9):

Type 5 (The Observer): Analytical, impartial, and know-how-focused. Prefer isolation for soaking up information, and talk really and may appearance guarded.

Type four (The Individualist): Expressive, expressive, and authenticity-pushed. Communicate mainly techniques, recognize actual connection, and can be liable to theatrical language.

Type 9 (The Peacemaker): Easygoing, adaptable, and war-averse. Seek not unusual ground, limit emotional response, and on occasion struggle to unique their very own beliefs.

Tips for Harmonious Communication:

Understanding Motivations: Recognize the easy goals and anxieties using each type's communication method.

Active Listening: Pay extremely good hobby not pleasant to the phrases, however additionally to the emotional undertones and underlying dreams.

Empathy and Validation: Acknowledge and recognize every splendid's viewpoints, despite the fact that they range from your non-public.

Direct and Clear Communication: Express your non-public wishes and mind freely and really, without blaming or accusations.

Focus on "We" Language: Shift from individual viewpoints to collaborative hassle-fixing, finding solutions that benefit each side.

Embrace Openness and Vulnerability: Create a comfortable environment for sharing emotional evaluations and troubles, improving connection and receive as actual with.

Celebrate Differences: View your Enneagram types as complementary, embracing the numerous tendencies and evaluations every one offers to the partnership.

Marriage Specific Considerations:

Shared Values and Goals: Discuss and assemble congruence on fundamental existence picks, parenting practices, and financial goals.

Conflict Resolution: Develop healthful war selection approaches that cope with underlying needs and issues, in choice to attention on blame or defensiveness.

Celebrating Each Other: Express gratitude to your associate's distinguishing features and contributions, encouraging connection, and high great reinforcement.

Continuous Learning: Remain open to increase and private development, embracing the Enneagram as a tool for self-interest and extended information of your relationship.

Remember, that is only a start line. Exploring resources, attending seminars, or maybe seeking out professional guidance can also moreover similarly expand your verbal exchange skills and growth your attention of every one of a kind's Enneagram kinds. By embracing open conversation, empathy, and a choice to study and growth, you could set up a a fulfillment and glad partnership, stronger by way of the one-of-a-kind viewpoints and tendencies of your specific Enneagram mixture.

Chapter 3: Navigating Conflict With The Enneagram

Conflict is inescapable in each dating, however knowing you and your partner's Enneagram kinds can also provide you with important competencies for coping with it constructively. Here's how every variety handles conflict of words, together with recommendation for resolving it correctly:

The Assertive Triad:

Type eight (The Challenger): Crave directness and honesty. Value open debates and can appearance confrontational.

Tips: Listen cautiously, validate their problems, put off defensiveness, and cope with win-win answers.

Type 7 (The Enthusiast): May avoid war of words or reduce hurdles. Can develop frustrated with protracted debates.

Tips: Slow down, understand their challenges, provide clean replies, and avoid negativity and ultimatums.

Type 3 (The Achiever): Focused on answers and fast achievements Can be disdainful of feelings.

Tips: Allow room for expressing thoughts, cope with essential troubles past floor solutions, and be affected man or woman with slower communique strategies.

The Feeling Triad:

Type 2 (The Helper): Prioritize concord and might push aside their personal pursuits to save you dispute.

Tips: Encourage kids to talk their necessities as it must be, avoid taking gain of their helpfulness, and deliver comfort and admiration.

Type 1 (The Reformer): Seek justice and can come to be crucial or perfectionistic in battle of phrases.

Tips: Acknowledge their need for justice, supply interest to man or woman troubles rather than blame, and provide particular treatments.

Type 6 (The Loyalist): Need balance and protection, may want to possibly revel in uncomfortable or reluctant amid disagreement.

Tips: Offer smooth conversation and realistic objectives, deal with their anxieties and aid their concerns, and create collaborative hassle-solving.

The Thinking Triad:

Type 5 (The Observer): May flee from war of words or approach it notably. Can problems in expressing feelings.

Tips: Create a secure environment for sharing, be affected man or woman with their processing time, and encourage them to voice their desires past rationality.

Type four (The Individualist): Seek authenticity and may come to be theatrical or emotionally responding in dispute.

Tips: Validate their sentiments; keep away from disparaging their research, and deliver emotional assist with unique policies.

Type 9 (The Peacemaker): Avoid disagreement and may war to installation their perspectives Can emerge as apathetic in debate.

Tips: Encourage children to speak their goals, actively pay attention and guide their feature, and set up weather in which youngsters experience comfortable to disagree.

General Tips for All Types:

Focus on "We" Language: Shift from person viewpoints to collaborative trouble-fixing, finding answers that advantage every side.

Practice Active Listening: Pay exquisite attention to each verbal and nonverbal symptom, and apprehend and affirm their emotions without judgment.

Respect Each Other's communiqué Styles: Recognize their desired strategies of processing information and expressing oneself, and alter your conversation correctly.

Focus on Underlying Needs: Look within the once more of the floor problem to find out the principle anxieties or needs generating the war of phrases.

Embrace Openness and Vulnerability: Create a secure environment for discussing emotions and problems, generating stronger connection and data.

Remember, dispute resolution is a know-how that takes exercise and staying power. By accepting the Enneagram as a device for self-interest and empathy, you could empower yourself to govern problems constructively, expand your relationship, and assemble a platform for mutual understanding.

Practical Journal

Reflecting on your Enneagram kind, what specific behaviors or terms out of your accomplice usually reason your reaction in struggle conditions?

Is it their directness, their retreat, or their wish to avoid emotions?

Once identified, discover real measures you can take to control your personal response and remain calm at the same time as those triggers emerge.

Choose a tough former disagreement alongside facet your associate. Reimagine the problem via the prism of your and your companion's Enneagram sorts.

What unique communique strategies would possibly you have got deployed, given your recognition of each exclusive's necessities and verbal exchange styles, to acquire a more inexperienced and right preference?

By taking the time to ruminate over those issues, you could gather deeper insights into your precise triggers and set up proactive abilities for handling battle, ultimately developing a calmer and linked dating.

BUILDING EMOTIONAL INTIMACY ACROSS ENNEAGRAM TYPES

Emotional intimacy, that unique circumstance of vulnerability and real connection is the lifeblood of every high-quality courting. But with nine specific Enneagram types at play, finding the direction to intimacy can also additionally appear like crossing a hard emotional terrain. Worry no longer, love seekers! Let's delve on the precise wishes and worrying situations of each kind, giving techniques to set up bridges and nurture proper emotional connections.

The Assertive Triad:

Type 8 (The Challenger): These sturdy dad and mom preference actual honesty and abhor vulnerable factor.

Building Intimacy: Show them you can manage their passion, partake in fierce debates, and include their need for control. Be frank together with your personal emotions, and do now not turn away from debate. (Think volcanic heat springs - violent, however profoundly remodeling!)

Type 7 (The Enthusiast): Playful and enthusiastic, Sevens yearn for shared opinions and dread stagnation.

Building Intimacy: Join their adventures, embody lightheartedness, and preserve topics new. Be affected man or woman with their short interest, and set up a secure place for emotional intensity while they may be ready. (Picture a frenzied dance party under a starry sky — exhilarating and ever-converting!)

Type 3 (The Achiever): Driven and intention-orientated, Threes dread shortcomings and preference reward.

Building Intimacy: Celebrate their triumphs, express sincere thank you for their efforts, and be a beneficial accomplice of their goals. Encourage them to sluggish down and engage emotionally, past successes. (Imagine accomplishing the top of a mountain collectively — thrilling and anchored in shared achievement!)

The Feeling Triad:

Type 2 (The Helper): Empathetic and being concerned, Twos dread rejection and prioritize others' dreams.

Building Intimacy: Reassure them of your affection, highlight their dreams as nicely, and encourage them to articulate their private dreams. Show thanks for their resource and offer a place for them to accept. (Think of a nice candlelight bathtub spent together with your sweetheart - serene and soothing!)

Type 1 (The Reformer): Conscientious and principled, Ones regardless of injustice and looking for excellence.

Building Intimacy: Engage in huge discussions, apprehend their immoderate aspirations, and be aware about their ideas. Show them your preference for personal development and consist of their enthusiasm for a higher network. (Picture a quiet communicate by means of a heart — thoughtful and primarily based in commonplace beliefs!)

Type 6 (The Loyalist): Security-looking for and collaborative, Sixes dislike desertion and need comfort.

Building Intimacy: deliver constant useful resource, deliver smooth conversation, and include them in choice-making. Be empathetic with their tension and installation a snug area for addressing fears. (Imagine growing a strong cabin together - solid and packed with mutual believe!)

The Thinking Triad:

Type five (The Observer): Analytical and impartial, Fives despise interruption and treasure isolation.

Building Intimacy: Respect their want for region, take part in exciting highbrow exchanges, and provide non-intrusive assist. Be affected character with their no longer on time emotional improvement and take delivery in their specific perspective. (Picture a peaceful library with soothing lighting, crowded with volumes and murmured talks –

intellectually exciting and privy to personal area!)

Type 4 (The Individualist): Expressive and authenticity-driven, Fours dread emotional vacancy and desire real connection.

Building Intimacy: Be their emotional sounding board, take part in revolutionary expression collectively, and respect their precise memories. Celebrate their depth and create an area for vulnerability with out judgment. (Imagine a passionate dance beneath a typhoon-crammed sky — emotionally excessive and profoundly intimate!)

Type 9 (The Peacemaker): Easygoing and conflict-averse, Nines dread separation and emphasize concord.

Building Intimacy: Draw them out softly, participate in quiet and wise talks, and provide a serene location for them to offer an reason in the back of their goals. Respect their name for for impartiality and provide substantiation of your emotional connection. (Think of a high-quality lake reflecting a smooth sky - calm and pleasantly associated!)

Remember, that is most effective a start line. Be open, inquiring, and adaptable as you find out the emotional landscapes of your specific Enneagram combination. Celebrate the variations, find out not unusual floor, and maximum

Practical Journal

Reflect to your Enneagram kind.

What specific concerns or fears come whilst you bear in mind getting into deeper emotional connection with your accomplice?

Can you describe any behavior or sports activities you behavior that may unknowingly purpose distance?

Brainstorm techniques to regularly erase the ones impediments and accept vulnerability to connect on a deeper level.

Imagine your ideal hideaway for shared emotional connection with your sweetheart.

What components will be present?

Would it is a hectic marketplace of shared critiques, a tiny library illuminated thru extremely good debate, or a serene lawn of fostered vulnerability?

Use this photo to find out mutual interests, communique skills, and emotional expressions that develop deeper connection and convey your quality courting to reality.

Remember, developing emotional connection is a ordinary way. These suggestions are most effective stepping stones to encourage your studies and experimentation. Embrace the beauty of your unique Enneagram dynamic and encompass the growing depths of your dating!

LOVE LANGUAGES AND ENNEAGRAM TYPES

The Enneagram uncovers our crucial motives and fears, while the 5 love languages - words of affirmation, acts of issuer, first-rate time, gives, and bodily touch – tell us how we love to offer and collect love. By weaving these frameworks collectively, we can also additionally get startling insights about our very own and our associate's emotional landscapes, allowing deeper information and enriching our relationships.

Exploring the Interplay

The Assertive Triad:

Type 8 (The Challenger): Often desires phrases of encouragement that apprehend their strength and enthusiasm Acts of service that mirror real help can also resonate. Their love language should display as specific confessions of adoration or deeds of authentic devotion.

Type 7 (The Enthusiast): Thrives on superb time full of shared pastimes and captivating interactions. They enjoy offers that advise clean reviews or creative impulses. Their love language might also involve unanticipated adventures, humorous gestures, or sharing precious recollections.

Type 3 (The Achiever): Values phrases of praise that well known their successes and promote their aspirations. Acts of provider that lessen their weight may additionally enhance their appreciation. Their love language should comprise joint purpose-putting, celebrating successes, or expressing pride in their achievements.

The Feeling Triad:

Type 2 (The Helper): Responds strongly to phrases of encouragement showing gratitude and compassion Acts of company that exhibit love and being involved are their lifeline. Their love language should entail looking beforehand to dreams, showering their accomplice with attention, or giving sacrificial help.

Type 1 (The Reformer): Appreciates phrases of thank you that widely known their labor and devotion to justice. Quality time hooked up sizable talks resonates strongly. Their love language could entail taking part in moral conflicts, turning in critical steering, or constructing a shared imaginative and prescient for a higher society.

Type 6 (The Loyalist): Feels comforted thru phrases of praise that suggest loyalty and affection Acts of company that advocate dependability and collaboration are vital. Their love language can entail expressing ordinary assist, providing a consistent location for vulnerabilities, or building lifestyles of shared sporting activities and rituals.

The Thinking Triad:

Type five (The Observer): Appreciates great time installed highbrow hobbies and severe talks. Words of reward respecting their insights and information resound. Their love language can also entail sharing insightful discoveries, taking part in intellectual verbal exchange, or giving a place for impartial inquiry collectively.

Type four (The Individualist): Values terms of reward that reaffirm their precise recollections and emotional depth. Quality time spent knowledge shared pursuits and weaknesses is critical. Their love language can also additionally want to include unusual displays of love, strong emotional talks, or respecting their companion's honesty.

Type nine (The Peacemaker): Responds truly to acts of provider that display concord and thoughtfulness. Words of encouragement that carry thankfulness for his or her soothing presence are valued. Their love language can encompass growing a serene surroundings, giving moderate guide, and expressing admiration for their quiet staying strength.

However, spotting your and your associate's Enneagram types and most vital love languages can be a useful tool to:

Decode Communication: Recognize how each type expresses and perceives love in another manner

Bridge Gaps: Speak your companion's decided on love language to revel in surely preferred and revered.

Deepen Intimacy: Tailor your phrases, moves, and gestures to boom your specific emotional connection.

Resolve Conflict: Approach conflicts with empathy and data, respecting each specific's desires.

Ultimately, merging Enneagram and love languages gives a rich tapestry for understanding your companion's particular emotional map. By expressing their language of affection and acknowledging their individual approach of feeling emotional connection, you can pave the door for a deeper, greater huge relationship.

Remember, love is a journey, not a holiday spot. Keep exploring, hold learning, and maintain constructing the cute dance of information among you and your partner.

Chapter 4: Navigating Values And Priorities

The Enneagram exposes our essential drives and fears, setting up our values and desires in lifestyles. In relationships, appreciating those versions can be a important device for managing battle, strengthening statistics, and growing a strong basis of understand and admiration for every other's character perspectives.

Here's a test how diverse Enneagram types prioritize values, along with pointers for overcoming any versions:

Assertive Triad:

Type eight (The Challenger): Justice, honesty, energy, independence, manipulate.

Tips: Embrace wholesome discourse, promote their preference for autonomy, keep away from strength clashes, verify their energy and exuberance.

Type 7 (The Enthusiast): Freedom, spontaneity, amusement, range, optimism.

Tips: create flexibility, create shared critiques, provide chances for satisfaction, avoid confining their free spirit, and laud their enthusiasm for existence.

Type three (The Achiever): Success, accomplishment, efficiency, popularity, picture.

Tips: Support their goals, have amusing triumphs, inspire artwork-existence balance, take delivery of their exhilaration, avoid criticizing their attention on seems.

Feeling Triad:

Type 2 (The Helper): Love, connection, service, selflessness, appreciation.

Tips: Acknowledge their generosity, particular thank you, promote self-care, avoid taking gain in their helpfulness, and validate their yearning to be preferred.

Type 1 (The Reformer): Integrity, fairness, betterment, idealism, accuracy.

Tips: Engage in meaningful talks, receive their aspirations, create not unusual dreams for suitable transformation, keep away from criticizing their perfectionism, and recognize their power of will to ethics.

Type 6 (The Loyalist): Security, loyalty, community, manual, and belonging.

Tips: Offer consolation, growth regular exercise routines, useful resource clean conversation, keep away from raising their worry, apprehend their devotion to relationships.

Thinking Triad:

Type 5 (The Observer): Knowledge, facts, privacy, independence, competence.

Tips: encompass their desire for isolation, have interaction in cerebral talks, avoid overwhelming them with emotional intensity, accept their insights and facts.

Type 4 (The Individualist): Authenticity, intensity, originality, emotional expression, individuality.

Tips: Validate their feelings, provide area for introduction, appreciate their originality, avoid ignoring their sensitivity, and apprehend their depth and honesty.

Type 9 (The Peacemaker): Harmony, consolation, peace, popularity, connection.

Tips: Foster calm conditions, restrict dispute escalation, sell open communication, take delivery in their name for for neutrality, and recognize their strength to construct togetherness.

General Tips for Navigating Differences:

Open Communication: Discuss values freely and genuinely, appreciating each particular's intentions.

Empathy and Respect: Recognize the validity of each different's critiques, although they variety out of your very non-public.

Find common Ground: Identify shared ideals you can every consist of and prioritize.

Negotiate and Compromise: Find solutions that recognize both sides' goals and targets.

Celebrate Differences: View them as a danger for improvement and gaining knowledge of, improving your reference to a larger angle.

Seek Professional Help: Consider couples treatment or Enneagram training for extra assist.

Remember, relationships are a dance of improvement and information. By embracing the spectrum of values inside the Enneagram, you could assemble a colourful tapestry of recognize, appreciation, and harmonious connection.

Practical Journal

What drives you, motivates you, and offers you a sense of because of this?

Consider how those concepts also can moreover materialize for your ordinary behaviors, relationships, and lengthy-term targets.

Do any probable discrepancies along with your partner's thoughts spring to thoughts?

Imagine a scenario in which your values and your accomplice's (counting on their Enneagram type) come into war. For instance, your stress for chronic journey (Type 7) may additionally moreover assessment with their requirement for a constant normal (Type 6) Using your expertise of each special's beliefs and objectives, are attempting to find sparkling ideas or compromises that might bridge the distinction and produce a collectively happy final effects.

Remember, values are not static however may additionally adjust over the years thru each man or woman and shared research. As you navigate this surroundings together, hold the strains of conversation open, boom healthful battle choice, and admire the appropriate tapestry of values that complements your courting.

UNDERSTANDING PARENTING STYLES THROUGH THE LENS OF ENNEAGRAM

Parenting is a top notch, messy, and regularly virtually bewildering assignment. The Enneagram, with its nine unique character sorts, also can deliver useful insights on our herbal parenting techniques, strengths, and challenges. By recognizing your and your companion's Enneagram kinds, you could manage parenting problems greater correctly, assemble sturdy relationships with your youngsters, and create a joyous own family environment.

Let's observe the parenting behaviors of every Enneagram type:

The Assertive Triad:

Type 8 (The Challenger): Strong, protective, decisive, direct can be overprotective or dictatorial.

Strengths: Instills self warranty, fosters independence, and encourages addressing barriers head-on.

Challenges: Can be overbearing, problem with emotional openness, need to balance manage with take into account.

Type 7 (The Enthusiast): Fun-loving, energetic, flexible, hopeful Can be uneven or pretty tolerant.

Strengths: Creates a satisfied environment, stimulates revolutionary inquiry, teaches version.

Challenges: May war with field, prioritize their very own goals, want to set limits and exercises.

Type 3 (The Achiever): Goal-oriented, green, high-reaching, consequences-pushed. Can be relatively rigid or centered on accomplishment.

Strengths: Instills paintings ethic, promotes immoderate requirements, and pushes motive-placing and achievement.

Challenges: Can be essential, placed their very very own pastimes above children's desires, want to emphasize circle of relatives fine time.

The Feeling Triad:

Type 2 (The Helper): Supportive, type, empathic, attentive to others' wishes. Can be overindulgent or codependent.

Strengths: Creates a heat and stressful environment, builds robust emotional connection, and teaches empathy and compassion.

Challenges: May warfare with putting limits, prioritizing children's desires before their very very personal, need to emphasize self-care and emotional boundaries.

Type 1 (The Reformer): Conscientious, responsible, honest, and rule-abiding Can be excessively rigorous or perfectionistic.

Strengths: Teaches responsibility, instills robust values, promotes a ordinary and predictable surroundings.

Challenges: Can be harsh or important, decide upon hints over emotional connection, want to integrate suggestions with flexibility and empathy.

Type 6 (The Loyalist): Secure, supportive, sincere, cautious Can be concerned or overprotective.

Strengths: Creates a safe and strong ecosystem, builds loyalty and self-discipline, indicates the significance of own family and guide.

Challenges: May war with letting pass, worry excessively about kid's protection, need to learn how to take delivery of as real with their kid's capabilities.

The Thinking Triad:

Type 5 (The Observer): Analytical, unbiased, informed, likes seclusion Can be emotionally aloof or disconnected.

Strengths: encourages self sufficient questioning, stimulates highbrow hobby, and generates a tranquil and quiet placing.

Challenges: May war with emotional expression, price intellectual hobby over emotional connection, want to stability isolation with family involvement.

Type 4 (The Individualist): Authentic, revolutionary, immensely empathic, emotionally expressive Can be grumpy or self-absorbed.

Strengths: Encourages progressive expression, acknowledges emotional opinions, and underlines the importance of honesty.

Challenges: May struggle with project, prioritize their personal emotional desires, and want to set up stability among self-expression and circle of relatives commitments.

Type 9 (The Peacemaker): Easygoing, high-quality, warfare-averse, seeks unification. Can be indecisive or avoidant.

Strengths: Creates non violent and quality surroundings, fosters collaboration and compromise, and teaches adaptability and hassle solving.

Challenges: May battle with saying no, avoid uncomfortable talks, and want to learn how to offer a cause of their non-public desires and ideals.

Remember, those are in truth essential outlines, and person variations upward thrust up inner every species. However, spotting you and your own family participants' Enneagram sorts can be a high-quality tool for:

Improving Communication: Recognize preferred conversation styles and change your approach successfully

Strengthening Bonds Foster connections by the use of acknowledging every first-rate's goals and reasons.

Navigating issues: Approach parenting problems with information and compassion, finding answers that paintings for everyone.

Setting Healthy Boundaries: Establish clean necessities and barriers while respecting person desires.

Growing Together: Use the Enneagram as a device for private and family development, analyzing from each one of a kind and improving individual strengths.

Ultimately, successful parenting isn't always approximately fitting right into a selected mildew, however approximately enhancing your approach to reflect the specific desires of your kids.

Chapter 5: Sexuality And The Enneagram In Relationships

Intimacy in marriage goes beyond the emotional, embracing the location of physical and sexual connection. The Enneagram, with its 9 unique individual kinds, gives a fascinating prism thru which to assess person variances in sexual expression and its impact on marital intimacy. While no longer created as a whole manual to every kind's mattress room behavior, figuring out those underlying motives and concerns may additionally sturdy mild on dreams, communique techniques, and possible issues inside a marriage.

Exploring the Triads

The Assertive Triad:

Type 8 (The Challenger): Craves huge passion and manage, propelled by way of energy dynamics and directness Can be competitive or bossy.

Strengths: Confident, adventurous, takes initiative.

Challenges: Needs to balance electricity with vulnerability, recognize partner's goals and boundaries.

Type 7 (The Enthusiast): Seeks variety and revolutionary inquiry, prospers on uncertainty and surprise Can be inconsistent or harassed.

Strengths: Fun-loving, open-minded, keeps topics new.

Challenges: Needs to spend great time and deeper connection, stability discovery with emotional closeness.

Type three (The Achiever): Approaches sexuality with reason-oriented performance, trying to find final contact and affirmation Can be emotionally remote or targeted on effects.

Strengths: Driven, bold, appreciates sensual encounters.

Challenges: Needs to attach emotionally, put amusing earlier than ordinary performance, and tolerate vulnerability.

The Feeling Triad:

Type 2 (The Helper): Prioritizes partner's delight and success, usually sacrificing their very very own desires. Can be codependent or manipulative.

Strengths: Empathetic, being involved, centered on building a loving environment.

Challenges: Needs to set constraints, make clean their very personal aspirations, keep away from disregarding self-care.

Type 1 (The Reformer): Seeks order and ethical bounds, is probably reluctant and critical of their personal and associate's options Can be proscribing or judgmental.

Strengths: Conscientious, responsible, desires great connection.

Challenges: Needs to accept sensuality, lighten up manage, supply wishes virtually.

Type 6 (The Loyalist): calls for stability and emotional protection, goals reassurance and self perception. Can be concerned or avoidant of vulnerability.

Strengths: Loyal, supportive, desires closeness and connection.

Challenges: Needs to cope with problems, battle fears, balance safety with spontaneity.

The Thinking Triad:

Type 5 (The Observer): Values highbrow connection and information, may retreat emotionally or treasure isolation Can be indifferent or analytical.

Strengths: Can increase intellectually captivating connection, values verbal exchange and consider.

Challenges: Needs to mix intellectualism with sensuality, articulate thoughts actually, and have interaction physical.

Type 4 (The Individualist): Seeks real emotional connection and self-expression, values originality and honesty in relationships Can be grumpy or self-absorbed.

Strengths: Creative, passionate, dreams deep emotional closeness.

Challenges: has to stability emotional intensity with associate's expectations, prevent manipulation, deliver desires efficaciously.

Type nine (The Peacemaker): Avoids warfare of words and emotional depth, craves quiet and emotional stability Can be passive or detached.

Strengths: Easygoing, flexible, appreciates calm connection.

Challenges: Needs to begin and make clean needs, overcome fear of war of words, encompass emotional expression.

Remember, those are massive dispositions, but individual variances occur interior each employer. Additionally, societal and non secular elements have a vital function in increasing sexual expression.

Enhancing Marital Intimacy:

Open Communication: Talk freely and actually approximately sexual wishes, desires, and alternatives, providing a cushty climate for vulnerability.

Empathy & Understanding: Recognize and understand your associate's precise manner of expression and anticipated problems counting on their Enneagram type.

Celebrating Differences: View unique sexual expressions as a supply of range and inquiry, not a purpose of war

Seeking Support: Professional treatment or couples counseling can also deliver belief and solutions for managing problems and growing better relationships

Ultimately, a successful sexual connection in marriage is a chronic adventure of discovery and development. By knowledge your private and your partner's Enneagram kinds, you may engage on this journey with more self-awareness, empathy, and a readiness to include the cute dance of intimacy in its various incarnations.

Practical Journal

Reflecting to your Enneagram kind, what offers you pleasure and delight within the place of physical intimacy?

Do you desire journey and exploration (Type 7), deep emotional connection (Type four), or a feel of balance and endure in mind (Type 6)?

Explore particular pastimes, verbal exchange patterns, and likely weaknesses related to your type.

Based for your statistics of your companion's Enneagram type, how also can furthermore their mindset to sexuality range from yours?

Can you identify their preferred verbal exchange fashion, diploma of emotional connection, and any troubles they may face?

How are you able to adjust your technique to bridge the gap and create a at the identical time nice revel in?

Imagine a situation while your severa sexual tendencies or expectancies gift a problem in your marriage.

Could or not it's a lack of emotional connection (Type five), opposing levels of spontaneity (Type three & Type nine), or competing priorities amongst delight and overall performance (Type 8 & Type 2)?

Use your facts of every different's Enneagram kinds to create specific answers, verbal exchange styles, and strategies to address the trouble with empathy and understanding.

Remember, know-how sexuality through the Enneagram is a adventure of self-discovery and open communication. Be affected man or woman, be sincere, and embody the risk to find out each exclusive's remarkable desires and extend your relationship on all degrees. Happy exploring!

COUPLES GROWTH AND DEVELOPMENT WITH THE ENNEAGRAM

The Enneagram, with its 9 precise personality sorts, offers a effective lens for know-how ourselves and our relationships. In the context of marriage, know-how each your and your associate's Enneagram sorts may be a transformative device for building deeper connection, resolving disputes, and helping every precise's increase.

Growth and Development through the Triads

The Assertive Triad:

Type eight (The Challenger): Growth includes acknowledging weakness, reading to percentage energy, and growing emotional intelligence.

Couples Growth: Support every one-of-a-kind in expressing feelings truly, resolving battle constructively, and know-how each unique's limits.

Type 7 (The Enthusiast): Growth entails reaching stability amongst spontaneity and dedication, promoting deeper emotional connection, and growing emotional intensity.

Couples Growth: Create room for both journey and intimacy, nurture emotional openness, and beneficial useful resource every one of a kind in developing and attaining top notch goals.

Type 3 (The Achiever): Growth consists of spotting the cost of vulnerability and emotional connection, prioritizing self-care, and reaching stability amongst art work and relationships.

Couples Growth: Celebrate triumphs collectively, inspire sincere conversation approximately goals and feelings, and make room for absolutely anybody and shared objectives.

The Feeling Triad:

Type 2 (The Helper): Growth includes growing accurate boundaries, prioritizing self-care, and studying to just accept love and assist without guilt.

Couples growth: Communicate individual goals and aspirations virtually, growth a comfortable weather for each providing and receiving assist, and manual every extraordinary to reap non-public accomplishment.

Type 1 (The Reformer): Growth consists of accepting imperfection, reading to forgive oneself and others, and growing emotional flexibility.

Couples development: Practice reputation and forgiveness, price information and empathy above judgment, and create a supportive ecosystem for private increase.

Type 6 (The Loyalist): Growth consists of gaining self-self assurance, overcoming worry, and reading to don't forget their non-public judgment and instincts.

Couples Growth: Offer consolation and assist, stimulate honest communication about problems, and expand a foundation of don't forget and mutual recognize.

The Thinking Triad:

Type five (The Observer): Growth entails blending intellectualism with emotional expression, attractive with humans on a deeper stage, and shifting past their comfort zone.

Couples Growth: promote emotional openness, supply room for shared sports and stories, and guide every exclusive in taking possibilities and exploring new things.

Type four (The Individualist): Growth calls for finding stability amongst self-expression and emotional connection, cultivating self-compassion, and studying to govern relationships without manipulation.

Couples Growth Practice honest verbal exchange, come to be aware about each one-of-a-kind's emotions, and offer guide without judgment or manipulation.

Type nine (The Peacemaker): Growth consists of statistics their desires and aspirations, overcoming struggle avoidance, and embracing their very very personal unique voice.

Couples Growth: Encourage open verbal exchange approximately hopes and desires, offer a steady region for expressing thoughts and arguments, and recognize every other's robust factor.

Beyond the Triads:

Appreciating Differences: View your accomplice's Enneagram kind as a delivery of electricity and range, no longer a reason of opposition.

Effective Communication: Learn to speak successfully relying to your and your accomplice's desired communication styles.

Empathy and Understanding: Cultivate empathy and information for each one of a kind's intentions, concerns, and triggers.

Mutual Support: Support a similarly in private boom and development, honoring individual achievements and joint milestones.

Professional Guidance: Consider receiving expert help from an Enneagram-knowledgeable therapist or counselor to address stressful situations and decorate your recognition of your interpersonal dynamics.

Remember, development and development in a marriage is consistent journeys. The Enneagram is an vital tool for self-focus, verbal exchange, and expertise, but it isn't a magic bullet.Embrace the adventure, understand your precise connection, and receive the big capacity for improvement and deeper intimacy that the Enneagram can also additionally find out in your marriage.

Practical Journal

Reflecting on you and your companion's Enneagram sorts, pick out one area each wherein you can benefit from personal increase to your dating. For example, a Type 2 may also additionally look into developing appropriate barriers, on the identical time as a Type 8 may additionally focus on accepting vulnerability. Brainstorm severa activities or conduct you can examine as people and as a couple to beneficial useful resource your highlighted development areas.

Think of instances at the identical time as your high-quality Enneagram types contribute to verbal exchange problems. For example, a Type 1's hobby on accuracy cans evaluation with a Type 7's spontaneity. Role-play a normal state of affairs, the use of your information of each first rate's types to alternate your conversation patterns and craft a strategy that fosters mutual knowledge and handles the issue constructively.

Recall a specific time whilst you and your partner defeated a hurdle or reached a mutual intention, seeing it thru the prism of your Enneagram sorts.

Chapter 6: How The Enneagram Can Foster Enduring Love

The Enneagram, with its nine specific persona types, gives a fascinating prism via which to assess the touchy dance of extended-term partnerships. By studying our very own and our accomplice's essential motives, problems, and behaviors, we may additionally create deeper connections, overcome problems with extra ease, and collect a platform for enduring love.

Decoding the Dance:

Self-Knowledge: The Enneagram gives a reflect for self-meditated photograph, highlighting our strengths, flaws, and relational behaviors Recognizing our essential kind lets in us to expect obligation for our judgments and communication behavior.

Understanding Your partnership: Seeing your dating through the Enneagram lens lets in you to recognize their top notch angle, communique style, and emotional necessities. This promotes empathy and minimizes the opportunity of misinterpreting their behaviors or intentions.

Navigating Conflict Different Enneagram kinds have particular triggers and warfare techniques. Understanding those differences may additionally assist you forecast viable flashpoints and set up fine communique procedures for coping with problems.

Celebrating Differences the Enneagram depicts the rich tapestry of character interior a courting. Instead of perceiving differences as incompatibilities, you can learn how to apprehend every distinctive's severa abilties and viewpoints, enriching your courting.

Growing Together: Personal boom is a non-stop system, and the Enneagram can be a powerful tool for person and communal improvement. Supporting every special in seeing ability for growth and exploring non-public change enhances your connection and develops a not unusual direction closer to a more exciting union.

Exploring the Triads

The Assertive Triad:

Type 8 (The Challenger): Can benefit from analyzing to reveal vulnerability and navigate electricity contributors of the family greater constructively.

Type 7 (The Enthusiast): Needs to balance spontaneity with willpower and set up deeper emotional connection.

Type 3 (The Achiever): Should emphasize self-care, art work-lifestyles stability, and emotional vulnerability.

The Feeling Triad:

Type 2 (The Helper): Must deliver attention to growing appropriate boundaries and accepting self confidence without guilt.

Type 1 (The Reformer): Needs to take a look at forgiveness, take delivery of imperfection, and gain emotional flexibility.

Type 6 (The Loyalist): Should awareness on gaining self-self assure, conquering fear, and trusting their very own judgment.

The Thinking Triad:

Type five (The Observer): Needs to merge intellectualism with emotional expressiveness and interact with humans on a deeper degree.

Type four (The Individualist): Should offer interest to growing balance among self-expression and emotional connection, operating toward self-compassion, and dealing with relationships with out manipulation.

Type 9 (The Peacemaker): attempts to apprehend their desires and aspirations, overcome conflict avoidance, and embody their one in every of a kind voice.

Beyond the Triads:

Communication is Key: Mastering open and sincere communication based totally totally on every other's selected methods creates agree with and improves mutual know-how.

Empathy and Compassion: Cultivating empathy on your companion's reasons and anxieties increases your relationship and lets you cope with problems with understanding.

Shared Values and dreams: Defining your shared values and prolonged-time period aspirations offers a sense of reason and path, allowing stability and fulfillment inner your partnership.

Mutual Support and Encouragement: Supporting every distinctive's man or woman and not unusual goals deepens your relationship and recognizes every one in every of a kind's distinct skills.

Professional Guidance: Consider receiving expert assist from an Enneagram-informed therapist or counselor to dig deeper into your person and relational dynamics, especially even as experiencing extreme problems.

Remember, the Enneagram is not a deterministic blueprint, however a compass giving direction and self-cognizance. Embrace the street of information yourself and your partner, consist of the precise dance of your relationship, and allow the Enneagram to carry together a tapestry of lasting love and deep connection to your lengthy-term journey together.

Practical Journal

Reflect in your and your companion's Enneagram kinds.

How do your crucial dreams and weaknesses switch into your techniques of expressing and receiving love?

Can you pinpoint how your Enneagram kinds can also moreover furthermore make you revel in loved in a few other ways?

Brainstorm techniques to adjust your love expressions to connect to every distinct's character desires, making sure your adventure collectively is packed with the language of your hearts.

Recall a present day-day war for your dating Using your attention of your and your partner's Enneagram kinds, find out the triggers and conversation styles at play.

Could seeing those features have helped method the trouble in a wonderful way?

Explore strategies for mediating future disagreements constructively, depending to your Enneagram insights to bridge the gap and assemble answers that recognize every your goals.

Imagine your extended-time period objective on your connection.

What hobbies and desires do you need to carry out together?

How may moreover your particular capabilities, as determined with the beneficial aid of your Enneagram sorts, make contributions to putting in this not unusual future?

Brainstorm practical techniques to help each one-of-a-type's personal development trips, connecting your particular paths to create a extra colourful and exciting tapestry of love and accomplishment as you flow ahead hand-in-hand.

Chapter 7: The Hidden Passageways Of Life

Ever puzzled why a few human beings seem to have it all decided on the identical time because the relaxation mother and father are left scratching our heads? Is there a hidden roadmap they've determined? Well, the answer is each smooth and complex—there's a treasure map, okay, but it's now not hidden in a few historical cave. It's coded proper internal you. Imagine being the hero of your personal existence's journey, like an Indiana Jones however of the spirit, armed with understanding and guided by numbers.

Think of it this way: you're like an undiscovered manuscript filled with captivating testimonies and existence-converting secrets. But to spread the ones pages, you've had been given to do greater than without a doubt skim through. This takes us on a adventure once more in time, about 5,000 years again, to the length even as the Vedas had been written. These historical texts gave us something astonishingly enduring—

Vedic Numerology. It's not surely counting or doing math; it's the universe's personal language, one which's been there for the purpose that sunrise of time.

Now, don't hold in thoughts this a few quick weekend retreat to 'find out yourself'. Nah, this is the remaining avenue journey of your life. You may be everywhere—in the middle of a bustling crowd or by myself alongside facet your mind on a quiet beach—at the equal time as an perception would possibly strike you want a lightning bolt. That's the power of understanding your numbers or greedy the Enneagram frameworks; they're the signposts for your non-public journey, your inner GPS. The interesting element is, lifestyles will become an unfolding mystery in that you are each the detective and the enigma. Every revelation gives a modern-day day twist for your private saga, establishing up pathways you didn't even recognize existed. The closer you get to cracking the code of your very very own complexities, the more life opens up in strategies you in no way expected—be it in relationships, career, or your private boom.

But preserve your horses! This isn't a 'treatment it and it's carried out' type of puzzle. Oh no, the extra you dig, the extra you find out—a labyrinth of questions, wonders, and positive, a few inevitable demanding situations. It's the longest-walking display with the maximum fascinating plot, and you are the movie star.

So, ready to crack the number one clue? Strap in for this in no way-finishing saga wherein the script maintains converting however the hero—certain, that's you—remains at its exciting coronary heart. And you'll fast locate which you're a far more riveting individual than you ever gave yourself credit score for. How's that for a gripping first financial disaster?

Your adventure via information human nature is like walking via an historic, never-finishing library. Each e-book is penned through philosophers, sages, and current-day scientists who’ve passed down their data for generations. They’ve filled the library with their teachings, from the metaphysical mantras of the Vedas to the mental blueprints of Freud and Jung. But amongst those countless volumes, there’s a unique segment— guidebooks, if you'll—that have a right away, regular effect: Enneagram and Vedic Numerology.

You can do not forget the Enneagram as a guide written through manner of an expert trekker for a mountain excursion. This trekker is aware about every twist, turn, and slippery slope. The e-book tells you no longer most effective approximately your personal trekking style—whether or not or now not you pace earlier, take it easy, or want to forestall and revel in the view—however additionally the way you have got interplay collectively with your fellow trekkers. Why do you react as you do at the same time as you’re exhausted or while you hit a roadblock? The Enneagram offers the understand-the manner to navigate the ones human terrains.

Next to it sits the guidebook of Numerology, reputedly scribbled by way of the usage of way of a sage who's spent years under the banyan tree in deep meditation. Even although we've got a handful of various faculties of numerology from the historic civilizations, we will especially look at the Chaldeans and the Indian Vedic numerologies in this ebook. It whispers to you that your shipping numbers and call are like a cosmic QR code. They unveil your natural capabilities and your existence's reason, but in addition they arrive up with practical advice.

Don't get me wrong; those aren't shortcuts to enlightenment or self-reputation. Rather, hold in mind them as available equipment for your every day existence toolbox. Want to be a better chief at art work? These can help. Trying to understand what makes your accomplice tick? These offer clues. From shaping your personal relationships to knowledge societal dynamics, the ones are practical lanterns lights up your path in an in any other case dark cave.

And just a phrase of warning – this e-book is definitely a primary step in the direction of all the subjects we discover proper here. We deliver it to you as an appetizer earlier than the seven-course meal that you want to have via persevering with the spirit and quest for this expertise. What I am looking for to do right here is virtually to expose you a trailer of what you can accumulate via those structures. Watching the show in its complete is every distinct large journey! The library of human know-how is expansive, and at the same time as many books offer grand theories, those particular guidebooks serve the instant, concrete dreams of your each day life. Will you pick them up and have a look at them, or allow them to gather dirt at the shelf? The subsequent bankruptcy, as they say, is yours to install writing. Are you organized?

Chapter 8: The Enneagram

The Enneagram isn't surely a fleeting style that has caught the overall public's interest; it's an extended-reputation system that delves deep into human man or woman. The device's roots stretch an extended way back, borrowing from severa highbrow traditions—from the philosophical musings of historic Greece, the spiritual know-how of Egypt, or even the metaphysical insights from our very personal Indian subcontinent. This medley of impacts showcases the Enneagram's not unusual attraction, proving that the look for knowledge human nature transcends time and place.

The name Enneagram comes from the Greek: Ennea is the Greek phrase for 9 and Gramma way a few issue that's drawn or written.

So, what makes this historic gadget resonate with current-day psychology? It's all approximately practicality once a manual for religious seekers, the Enneagram these days has been tailored to the modern-day generation by using the usage of the use of visionaries like Claudio Naranjo, Don Richard Riso, and Russ Hudson. These cutting-edge torchbearers have repurposed it into a scientific tool, used for demystifying the regularly-baffling complexities of human behaviour. This transformation owes a good buy to Oscar Ichazo, a man who acted as a conduit among the Enneagram's historic roots and its current-day programs. Ichazo took this historic information and injected it with a dose of intellectual relevance, rescuing it from the chance of becoming a ancient footnote.

Now, this isn't a tool limited to the chambers of psychologists or the pious corridors of non secular experts. Think of a examine room—a place wherein younger minds are moulded. Teachers armed with the Enneagram can decode the fantastic mastering types of their university university college students. It turns the observe room from a monologue right into a talk, from a one-length-fits-all version proper right into a numerous however unified studying environment.

And what approximately families? Every discern knows that elevating a infant doesn't encompass an education manual. But, with the Enneagram, it's almost as if you have a region guide to your little one's ever-changing temperament and emotional goals. Understanding why your toddler behaves in a selected manner can redesign the figure-infant courting from a war right into a journey of mutual discovery. The administrative center is every different battleground of contrasting personalities, in which the Enneagram proves profitable. This isn't pretty a good buy resolving conflicts; it's about constructing a hard and fast this is acquainted with and complements each exceptional's strengths and weaknesses. When a frontrunner can inform obligations to group participants based totally mostly on their inherent inclinations, the stop end result is a harmonious, extra inexperienced place of business. The software extends from the HR departments to the booths or even the boardrooms.

Now, permit's increase our gaze to the geographical regions of private relationships. The counsellor's office, frequently visible as a last inn for distressed couples, will become a place of revelation with the Enneagram. Through information one's accomplice's kind, the dynamics of a relationship can alternate; conflicts may be navigated, and new pathways of understanding can be solid. It's like having a translator for emotional language, making every associate's desires and expectancies extra legible to the opportunity.

The Enneagram has greater to offer. In the swiftly evolving vicinity of education, certain beforehand-wondering establishments are incorporating it into their pedagogy. By information the Enneagram kinds of college college students, curriculum builders are starting to tailor training in a more customized way. It's now not truly the priority depend that is considered; it's how every scholar will soak up and relate to the material. That's progressive. Remarkably, the

Enneagram has additionally found its way into the criminal machine. Legal specialists, curious approximately human motivation and behavior, have started out to use it as a supplementary lens. It's no longer about proving innocence or guilt however approximately know-how the layers of human psychology that could affect movements. It offers a nuanced attitude that may be useful in complex prison court times.

The Enneagram's spiritual roots should not be forgotten every. Numerous spiritual leaders and companies are embracing it as a manner of personal development. It's turning into increasingly more commonplace to discover Enneagram workshops being completed in monasteries, church buildings, and spiritual retreats. This convergence of era and spirituality indicates the device's adaptability and wide-attaining relevance. Another widespread point is that the Enneagram isn't always static; it's an evolving framework. As greater research are accomplished and further information analysed, anticipate to appearance some refinements. But the center will stay—the essential purpose of understanding human nature for progressed coexistence will remain its popularity.

So, the Enneagram isn't always only a tool that has been exceeded down through the annals of information; it’s a dwelling, respiration framework that continues to comply and locate new packages. From classrooms and living rooms to organization offices and jail chambers, it has showed to be a useful asset. With roots deeply planted in historic knowledge and branches that reap out to understand cutting-edge complexities, the Enneagram serves as an evolving guide for humanity. The Enneagram is not most effective a theoretical concept; it is a practical device for each person interested in information the difficult mosaic of human person. With its multi-faceted programs and enduring relevance, it stays a robust and pretty useful gadget for non-public and societal properly-being.

Ancient Beginnings and Early Influence

The Enneagram is an charming assignment, not least as it sparks debates that attain throughout time and area, connecting historical civilizations like Greece and India to our modern. It's like a river whose deliver we're not pretty superb of, but whose tributaries we understand. Yet it's tough to aspect precisely to wherein it all started what combination of ideologies and philosophies gave upward push to this tricky system that tries to decode the mysteries of human behaviour.

In historical Greece, Pythagoras stands as a crucial hyperlink to the Enneagram. He is widely reliable for his contributions to mathematics and geometry but additionally had a profound hobby in spirituality. Pythagoras spent a large quantity of time in Heliopolis, Egypt. This metropolis changed proper right into a religious hub well-known for the worship of the Ennead, a set of 9 distinguished deities in Egyptian mythology.

During his live, it's possible that he encountered the foundational thoughts that could later shape the Enneagram. In addition to the Ennead, the concept of 'nine' holds special significance in Greece via the Nine Muses—the goddesses of the humanities, literature, and technological understanding. Just due to the fact the Ennead covers a giant spectrum of life's elements; the Nine Muses embody severa domain names of human creativity and information.

Switching our popularity to India, the land with rich Vedic traditions gives a few other lens to view the Enneagram. Vedic philosophy has a longstanding records with numerology, geometry, and astrology. Numbers in India are not simply digits; they bear a philosophical and non secular importance. This is specifically putting in Vedic astrology, wherein celestial positions are interpreted through complex geometric designs. The Indian exercising of assigning extra meaning to numbers echoes with the Enneagram's categorization of human personalities.

Now, allow’s return to historical Egypt to characteristic every different layer to our expertise. The Egyptians, mainly in Heliopolis, worshipped the Ennead, frequently known as the Great Ennead, that may be a organization of nine gods and goddesses who've been pretty respected in Egyptian folklore. These divine beings had been mainly worshipped in the town of Heliopolis. Atum, the sun god, is on the apex of this pantheon, followed through using using his offspring Shu and Tefnut. The lineage keeps with Shu and Tefnut’s youngsters, Geb and Nut, and in addition extends to their progeny—Osiris, Isis, Set, and Nephthys. Sometimes, Horus the Elder, a high-quality model of the falcon deity and no longer to be confused with Osiris and Isis’s son, is likewise blanketed within the Ennead. Just much like the nine Muses in Greece, the Ennead in Egypt represented a multi-faceted view of human studies and feelings. It wouldn’t be a long way-fetched to think that Egyptians may have considered this structure as a guide for navigating the maze-like complexities of human behaviour.

From Egypt, it made severa stops, as even though on a grand voyage—touching base with various spiritual and spiritual companies, every including its hue to the Enneagram's already colorful canvas. It placed its way into mystical Judaism, Christian doctrines, Islamic teachings, Taoist philosophy, Buddhist thoughts, and again to historical Greek ideologies. Each perception tool folded it into their teachings, enriching its form and making it as diverse as it's far these days. So, in case you think about it, the Enneagram isn't simply a tool or a device; it's greater like a palimpsest written over centuries, wherein each community has left its indelible mark.

Let's deliver in a greater modern-day take. In his ebook "The Sacred Enneagram: Finding Your Unique Path to Spiritual Growth", Christopher Heuertz indicates that the Enneagram may additionally have roots even past the Jewish and Christian narratives, increasing its sphere to a extra common, mystic realm. Here, Heuertz gives a nod to Beatrice Chesnut, who increases the element that the Enneagram's origins is probably embedded in texts that are but to be discovered, locations that are yet to be explored. Interestingly, Heuertz refers to Homer's "The Odyssey", in which the hero Odysseus traverses through nine one-of-a-kind lands, each teeming with particular disturbing situations and characters. The correlation amongst these 9 worlds and the Enneagram's 9 sorts is without a doubt too apparent to dismiss. Could or not it's far that the awareness of the Enneagram is ageless, its standards conventional? Heuertz seems to suppose so, arguing that the textual content turn out to be designed to persuade its readers inside the course of a profound journey of self-discovery. However, and this is in which the plot thickens, not absolutely everyone is purchasing for into this idea. Critics argue that the theories placed forth with the aid of way of Heuertz and Chesnut are not grounded in massive studies. They caution toward reading too much into historic texts, maintaining the hazard of projecting present day constructs onto them. Simply placed, even because it's tempting to view the Odyssey as a coded guidebook to statistics the Enneagram or the human psyche, we need to tread carefully.

One phrase of caution earlier than we near this concern matter — the Enneagram has had its percent of darkish days There have been durations even as it became twisted to match dubious notion structures, now and again even getting used for manipulative capabilities. But in recent times, it stands redeemed, employed as a optimistic approach to foster personal increase and enhance interpersonal relationships. The Enneagram has as a end result evolved, losing its mystical, esoteric cloak to put at the greater pragmatic attire of psychological profiling.

So, as you step once more and take a look at the winding course the Enneagram has journeyed, you discover a story this is many things —mysterious, enriching, controversial, but in no way stupid. Like a exquisite ancient record, it presents more questions than solutions, urging us to preserve exploring. The Enneagram, because of this, is not most effective a replicate reflecting our man or woman identities; it's a window presenting a glimpse into the collective knowledge and follies of human civilization across some time. And the view, I ought to say, is pretty captivating.

Modern Foundations and Cross-Cultural Synthesis

In the history of concept, some thoughts become crucibles wherein various cultural elements fuse to create a few component new, some component universally charming. The Enneagram is one such interesting concept. Its improvement over the 20 th century gives a tale full of intellectual voyages, arriving at a place where it stands nowadays as a bridge among ancient knowledge and cutting-edge records.

Let's first turn our gaze closer to George Ivanovich Gurdjieff, a name that even these days resonates in discussions about the

Enneagram. His characteristic become not that of a direction-breaking writer but greater of a connector who added disparate threads of Eastern and Western philosophies collectively. He discovered the Enneagram as a form of favored blueprint that could constitute cosmic laws and human dynamics. This became now not just mere educational dabbling; Gurdjieff had a challenge to show that human expertise converges at some essential truths. The Enneagram, in his eyes, changed right into a photograph effective sufficient to illuminate the ones convergences.

Following this fascinating starting came Oscar Ichazo from Bolivia. A guy of profound getting to know, he channelled his sizeable-ranging studies into growing the Arica School. This college modified into not surely an organization however a platform wherein Ichazo have to percent a life-time's certainly worth of knowledge.

Chapter 9: Learning Enneagram

So you've picked up this e-book, intrigued via the Enneagram or Numerology. Let's be clean, that is your starting point, your advent to a worldwide that's each historic and and not using a result in sight charming. Think of it as popularity at the shore of a massive ocean you're approximately to discover. We're no longer diving into the deep end truly but; we're without a doubt dipping our feet inside the water to experience its temperature.

The Enneagram and its nine individual types provide an fantastic roadmap to expertise human behaviour. But right right here, we're most effective commencing on the primary leg of the journey. Imagine you're in a grand library. We'll skim thru the primary pages of a few intriguing books, making ready you for the sagas that lie earlier. In the equal way, this ebook is your starter bundle. It's like your first-ever cricket in form. You acquired't emerge as Don Bradman or Brian Lara proper away, but you'll examine the easy suggestions, a manner to hold the bat, and possibly even hit a few photos. And much like cricket permits you understand teamwork and method, right here you'll start to see recommendations of your very personal character coming to slight.

Becoming an expert in those mystical arts is a adventure, not a two-minute Maggi noodles recipe. Consider this ebook the primary few spices on your curry. It will add a few flavour, however there's lots greater to the dish. You'll participate in workshops, test extra books, and chat with those who anticipate in some other manner. It's like a laboratory wherein you perform little experiments to have a examine how numbers or individual sorts take place in real life. Understanding the labyrinth of the human thoughts is not any small mission. But hold in thoughts, that is a beginner's maze, simpler and smaller, designed to offer you a taste of the project beforehand. This e-book doesn't have all the solutions; instead, it shows you the way to begin asking the proper questions. It fingers you the primary few portions of a grand puzzle, leaving you curious to discover the relaxation.

So, within the massive ocean of the Enneagram or Numerology, hold in mind this your first step into the water. We'll take you via the preliminary laps, enough to get you hooked but leaving loads so that you can find out and find out on your very personal. Every grand tapestry started with a single thread, and each expert come to be as soon as a amateur. Now that we've set the level, are you prepared to take the ones first steps? Because the road beforehand, my buddy, is lengthy but fascinating, and this is where all of it starts offevolved offevolved. Shall we?

The Enneagram System

In the Enneagram framework, we come across nine specific persona types. Each of those sorts offers a completely unique lens thru which people view and engage with the world. Think of those as foundational building blocks that help us get a clearer expertise of human conduct and motivations. CLet's check what are the nine types of Enneagram.

Type 1 The Reformer : The Reformer is a perfectionist at coronary coronary heart. They are generally very disciplined and adhere to excessive moral necessities. They like subjects to be sincere and accurate. If you be conscious a person who maintains speakme approximately the "right way" of doing subjects, or who gets stressed whilst matters are chaotic or inefficient, you're likely encountering a Type One. They are those who strive for development continuously. Practitioners will discover it useful to recognition on amusing the perfectionistic dispositions of Type Ones.

Type 2 The Helper : These people are all about relationships and assisting others. They are frequently heat and nurturing. If a person is commonly there to lend a helping hand, places others' desires in advance than their personal, and appears to feed off social interactions, it's miles quite possible which you are coping with a Type Two. This type benefits from studying to installation boundaries and taking time for self-care.

Type three The Achiever : Highly fulfillment-driven, Type Threes are the overachievers in any commercial enterprise agency. They are purpose-orientated and don't like losing time. They will be inclined to be aggressive, focusing on recognition and photo. Spotting a Type Three is exceptionally smooth: search for ambition, a focus on fulfillment, and a capability for workaholism. Practitioners must help Threes slow down and respect their intrinsic well definitely really worth past accomplishments.

Type 4 The Individualist : People falling under this class are normally emotionally excessive and feature an inherent ability for drama. They take delivery of as proper with they may be particular and first rate. If someone maintains talking approximately their extraordinary views or feelings, has a tendency to get lost in daydreams, and loves exploring their internal international, you've possibly had been given a Type Four. Practitioners need to cause to ground the ones sorts inside the reality of commonplace human opinions, thereby mitigating emotions of being usually 'certainly one of a type'.

Type 5 The Investigator : Curiosity marks this type. Type Fives decide upon looking at from a distance and are normally introverted. They want to acquire statistics and frequently have know-how in sudden regions. A person who appears extra interested in thoughts or books than in social interactions can often be categorised as a Type Five. For this kind, practitioners need to attention on encouraging extra active engagement with the area.

Type 6 The Loyalist : If a person is constantly organized, questions the entirety, and has a bent to worry lots, they may be in all likelihood a Type Six. They frequently are in search of for steerage or suggestions to make experience of the arena. Practitioners will discover that Type Six individuals gain from mastering to keep in mind themselves and gaining self notion in their choice-making competencies.

Type 7 The Enthusiast : This is the type that loves to find out new opportunities. They are spontaneous and don't want to be constrained with the resource of schedules or guidelines. If you be conscious a person who is generally obsessed with the following big aspect and hates being bored, you've in all likelihood encountered a Type Seven. Practitioners want to assist Sevens to recognition and understand the prevailing second, instead of constantly seeking to the following large component.

Type eight The Challenger : Powerful and dominating, Type Eights take price of conditions. They are proactive and recognize a manner to get subjects accomplished. They often have a shielding streak. If you note a person who isn't afraid to unique their evaluations boldly and takes the initiative, you're likely managing a Type Eight. Practitioners can guide Eights in know-how the electricity of vulnerability.

Type 9 The Peacemaker : Lastly, Type Nines are easy-going and hate conflicts. They prefer to preserve the peace and are commonly pretty accommodating and open-minded. If you apprehend someone who is always averting conflicts and looks to go with what all of us else dreams, they might be a Type Nine. Practitioners have to help Nines to realise that their critiques and dreams are crucial too.

When we take a look at every man or woman kind in element, we unearth the center dispositions that outline it. This system enables in big approaches. First, it lets in us to discover more about ourselves. We emerge as aware about why we act in splendid techniques and what drives our movements. Second, it improves our interactions with others. When we apprehend the fundamentals of a person's person, we are able to communicate and collaborate greater efficiently. This is not just theoretical understanding; it has practical implications in every day existence. It becomes a beneficial guide for self-improvement and enables us better manipulate our relationships, be it at domestic, art work, or in social settings.

Remember, everybody is specific, and at the same time as those classes offer a useful framework, they'll be just that—frameworks. However, a pro practitioner can use this guide as a place to start to delve deeper into expertise their customers' or subjects' intellectual and emotional landscapes. Understanding the middle motivations and fears can offer profound insights into the the usage of forces at the lower back of each Enneagram kind's behaviours and actions. It's critical to bear in thoughts that each type possesses each strengths and limitations, and the Enneagram adventure is ready embracing the overall spectrum of human nature.

Let’s check out the center motivations and fears of each type:

Type 1

Core Motivation: Striving for integrity and development. Ones are pushed via a want to do what's proper, clearly, and ethical.

Core Fear: Fear of being corrupt, faulty, or morally wrong. Ones dread making mistakes or failing to meet their very personal excessive requirements.

Type 2

Core Motivation: Seeking love and appreciation. Twos are stimulated with the aid of a preference to be wished, valued, and cherished with the aid of supporting and helping others.

Core Fear: Fear of being unloved, undesirable, or rejected. Twos worry that in the event that they don’t meet others’ goals, they will lose their connections.

Type 3

Core Motivation : Striving for achievement and reputation. Threes are driven to gain dreams, gain popularity, and gift a superb image to the sector.

Core Fear: Fear of being worthless or a failure. Threes worry that without success or admiration, they're insignificant.

Type four

Core Motivation: Seeking identification and significance. Fours are inspired to discover their unique identity and enjoy deep, real emotions.

Core Fear: Fear of being mundane or normal. Fours worry that they lack a sense of identity and may be neglected.

Type 5

Core Motivation: Pursuing information and expertise. Fives are driven to accumulate statistics and insights, searching for to apprehend the sector around them.

Core Fear: Fear of being overwhelmed or invaded. Fives dread feeling incapable of handling their surroundings or being emotionally beaten.

Type 6

Core Motivation: Seeking protection and useful resource. Sixes are prompted through a need for safety, loyalty, and guidance in an uncertain international.

Core Fear: Fear of being unsupported or without steerage. Sixes fear approximately being abandoned or going through threats without assist.

Chapter 10: The Enneagram Symbol

A smooth but complexly effective geometry

Imagine watching on the Enneagram photograph, a apparently smooth but profoundly sizable layout. Within its complex styles lies a wealth of expertise that transcends time and way of life. This photograph no longer quality encapsulates the essence of our life however additionally acts as a portal to the ancient understanding structures which have long-established human knowledge for millennia. As we find out the importance of the Enneagram photo, we discover its deep roots in complicated geometries and numerous religious traditions, highlighting its role as a bridge a few of the beyond and the prevailing.

The Enneagram picture has been a topic of keen interest in the path of numerous disciplines and cultures. It's easy geometric shape—a circle with a triangle and hexad internal—has been a canvas for complex interpretations. The time period "Enneagram" is derived from Greek, wherein 'Ennea' way nine and 'gram' refers to a drawing or determine. Though the geometric shape is easy, the origins of this fascinating photograph are quite complicated and multifaceted.

Starting with the Pythagorean connection, there may be speculation that Pythagoras, the historical Greek mathematician and reality seeker, evolved the Enneagram image within the route of his time in Heliopolis. Heliopolis end up an ancient Egyptian metropolis stated for its pupils and libraries. Pythagoras, who believed that geometry modified right into a manner to apprehend the divine, would probable have conceptualized the Enneagram as a example of normal laws and harmonies.

Another principle factors to Christian mysticism. Early Christian monks and students have been idea to employ symbols just like the Enneagram in their theological research Though not precisely the Enneagram as we comprehend it, those symbols had been used as system for contemplation and knowledge the divine nature. Such a correlation suggests that the Enneagram photo may additionally have Christian roots or at least parallel traits interior Christian mysticism. The Jewish Kabbalah additionally presents a compelling perspective. Kabbalistic students emphasize the sacredness of numbers and geometric figures. In this lifestyle, the Tree of Life—a photograph with ten interconnected nodes—shares similarities with the Enneagram. Both symbols reason to represent the complexities of existence and the divine, making them kindred spirits inside the global of historical symbols. When it includes similarities with extraordinary symbols, the Enneagram bears a close to resemblance to one of a kind geometric constructs used at some point of historic cultures. For instance, the Sri Yantra in Hinduism, an complex layout of 9 interlocking triangles, stocks the 9-pointed form. The Borromean Rings, every other mathematical determine with 3 interlocking circles, additionally echo the topic of interconnectedness positioned in the Enneagram.

George Gurdjieff, a 20th-century religious teacher, reintroduced the Enneagram photo, however his hobby become extra on its cosmological implications. His interpretations were no longer aligned with any precise non secular or philosophical lifestyle but instead aimed to encapsulate famous necessities and laws governing the cosmos. Bolivian psychologist Oscar Ichazo changed into instrumental in giving the Enneagram image its contemporary highbrow twist, associating its 9 elements with precise human character developments. However, this paper concentrates on the Enneagram as a image, with out its mental interpretations.

The Enneagram photograph's complexity and adaptableness have made it a topic of interest inside the course of diverse fields collectively with spirituality, psychology, and commercial enterprise corporation approach. Over time, the photo has absorbed elements from super intellectual traditions, making it a multidimensional entity of test.

The Enneagram and the Pentagram

The pentagram, a five-pointed big call enclosed in a circle, has extended and sundry facts at some stage in one among a kind cultures. Originally visible in Mesopotamian writings spherical 3500 BCE, the image has taken on various roles and meanings through the years. In ancient Greece, the pentagram turned into called the "Pentalpha", made from 5 interlocking A-fashioned alphabets. It was a photo related to the goddess Hygeia, who represents health. In medieval times, The Christian Church adopted the pentagram as a shielding emblem.

Christian traditions interpreted the 5 elements because the five wounds of Christ. But with the passage of time, its interpretation developed—or as an opportunity, devolved—into being related to the occult and witchcraft, particularly at some level in the overdue medieval duration. Fast beforehand to the 20 th century, the pentagram has become an emblem in current spirituality, mainly Wiccan and Neopagan traditions. Here it's far seen as a illustration of the five elements: earth, water, air, hearth, and spirit, every represented via a point of the huge call. On the scientific issue, the pentagram is frequently highlighted for its geometric perfection. It consists of the Golden Ratio, a mathematical percent located in lots of herbal phenomena, making it a subject of interest not just for spiritual leaders but additionally for mathematicians and scientists.

The Enneagram, within the intervening time, is a photograph that features nine factors and is first-class seemed for its software in man or woman typing. Its roots are harder to hint however are frequently attributed to spiritual traditions like Sufism and early kinds of Christianity. The nine factors are seen as a guide to human nature and mental tendencies, offering a structured approach to self-statistics and personal boom.

Despite their notable origins and number one uses, the pentagram and the Enneagram percentage key thematic similarities. Both are concerned with the human adventure in the direction of stability and completeness. The pentagram, through its instance of elemental stability, emphasizes the brotherly love of factors and spiritual equilibrium, advocates for harmony in our relationship with the herbal global. The Enneagram, as a substitute, indicates that expertise and integrating extraordinary aspects of our person can result in a extra balanced and outstanding life. The religious and medical convergence of the Enneagram and the pentagram highlights their shared motive of uncovering the hidden layers of existence. Both symbols encourage self-cognizance, transformation, and an exploration of the complicated threads that weave together our character opinions and the more cosmos.

On a broader stage, each symbols trace at a famous order. Whether it is the mathematical precision of the Golden Ratio within the pentagram or the established typology of human nature within the Enneagram, the message is plain: our complex worldwide and difficult personalities are not random or chaotic but guided through underlying necessities that we are able to recognize and test in our lives. The pentagram and the Enneagram, at the same time as rooted in one-of-a-type traditions and applied in particular contexts, function complementary gadget for exploring the complexities of lifestyles, be it our relationship with the outside international or our internal psychological landscapes. They offer a established approach to facts the only of a type dimensions of human experience, drawing on each spiritual ideals and clinical principles.

Contrast with exclusive cultures

The Enneagram has piqued human interest with its certain geometric form and insightful take at the human psyche. It's thrilling to take a look at that this as an alternative present day-day concept stocks similarities with historic symbols like Padmas and Yantras, stemming from religious traditions together with Tantric, Buddhist, and Vedic philosophies.

The Saraswathi Yantra

In those ancient non secular pathways, the Padma, or the lotus flower, holds a big vicinity. The lotus is a photograph of purity and non secular enlightenment, illustrating a journey from the dimness of loss of statistics to the slight of understanding. The Enneagram serves a comparable purpose, providing a route for self-discovery and personal increase. Designed as a circle with nine factors, every problem symbolizes a first rate man or woman kind. Both the Padma and the Enneagram stress that real growth arises from acknowledging the hidden complexities within us, not in evaluation to the way a lotus flower rises thru muddy waters to bloom underneath the solar.

Transitioning to Yantras, those are complicated geometric designs rooted in Tantric and Vedic traditions. Intended as gadgets of meditation, Yantras serve to set up a link amongst human awareness and higher spiritual dimensions. They are appeared as encapsulations of cosmic energies and archetypal ideas. Similarly, the Enneagram operates as a geometric outline of the human psyche. It gives keen insights into how the mind and feelings characteristic. While Yantras serve as portals to divine focus, the Enneagram features as a gateway to a greater self-recognition and character development.

Among Yantras, the Sri Yantra sticks out for its geometric sophistication. It combines triangles, circles, and floral styles to create a balanced visible composition. This particular Yantra symbolizes the union of masculine and woman divine energies. At its center, nine interlocking triangles offer a holistic mind-set of the universe and the requirements inside the once more of advent. The number one thing, called the “bindu”, indicates the starting point of existence. Therefore, the Sri Yantra gives a targeted recognition for meditation, important practitioners in the direction of enlightened states of thoughts.

Sri Yantra

In Buddhism, Mandalas feature every different instance of sacred geometry corresponding to the Enneagram. Mainly applied in meditation, Mandalas intention to guide humans from a rustic of lack of information to enlightenment. Both Mandalas and the Enneagram underscore the cyclical nature of human lifestyles, implying that fluctuations are an inherent a part of the transformative journey.

The commonalities between the Enneagram, Padmas, and Yantras propose the presence of time-commemorated requirements at some stage in one-of-a-type religious frameworks. These symbols pass beyond mere innovative designs; they act as modern-day machine for fostering deeper self-know-how and religious growth. This connection solidifies the perception that the pursuit of spiritual enlightenment and self-recognition is a shared human experience. It's virtually truely worth recognizing that the Enneagram's resemblance to symbols like Padmas and Yantras signifies a sure solidarity in non secular explorations at some stage in numerous cultural landscapes. Identifying those common styles can display enduring truths which have stimulated human endeavours for hundreds of years.

Chapter 11: Inner Symphony Of Enneagram

The fascinating Centres of Intelligence and Wings

Enneagram typology, while on the entire targeted on unveiling the intricacies of man or woman personalities, additionally offers insights into the dynamics of relationships and compatibility among different types. This issue of the Enneagram taps into the wealthy surroundings of human interactions, dropping slight on how one-of-a-type personalities can harmonize, battle, and evolve together. Understanding compatibility in the context of the Enneagram includes spotting how numerous character sorts interact, have an effect on, and respond to every different.

While each kind possesses wonderful trends and inclinations, the ones traits can both supplement or project the ones of every exclusive type. This dynamic interplay is a key characteristic of the Enneagram's holistic attitude on human relationships.

One way the Enneagram addresses compatibility is through the concept of wings. Each Enneagram kind is thought to have adjacent types called wings. These wing types have an impact on a person's center type, along with depth and nuance to their person. For example, a Type 1 may additionally moreover have a Type 2 or Type nine wing. Understanding the wings of one's personal type can offer insights into ability areas of compatibility with neighbouring sorts.

Moreover, the Enneagram's lines of connection depict how differing types can circulate closer to the excellent traits of some different type at the same time as they are experiencing increase, and conversely, how they're capable to expose off horrific tendencies while beneath strain. This facts opens a window into how relationships can impact non-public increase and transformation. For example, a Type five, diagnosed for his or her analytical nature, may moreover display off characteristics of a greater healthy Type 8 (The Challenger) on the same time as growing, embracing assertiveness and movement.

Centres of Intelligence

In the Enneagram system, the centres of intelligence are one manner of categorizing and facts how particular personality kinds machine data, emotions, and evaluations. These centres are referred to as the Body Centre, the Heart Centre, and the Head Centre. Each centre corresponds to a particular way of perceiving and responding to the world, and people inside the equal centre frequently percentage advantageous sorts of behaviour, emotional reactions, and perception approaches.

The compatibility of various types additionally pertains to their centre of intelligence – the Body Centre, the Heart Centre, and the Head Centre Types within the equal centre frequently percent commonplace emotional and cognitive responses, which both could cause harmony or struggle. Exploring how those centres engage within relationships presents valuable insights into conversation patterns and capability regions of synergy.

1. Body Centre (Instinctive Centre) The Body Centre encompasses sorts Eight, Nine, and One. Individuals inner this centre has a tendency to be more in contact with their bodily sensations and instincts. They depend upon their gut feelings and bodily cues to navigate the area. They frequently react instinctively to situations and prioritize motion. This centre is associated with problems of manage, anger, and instinctual responses.

Type Eight: Focus on manipulate, energy, and autonomy. Can be assertive and protecting but might also war with vulnerability.

Type Nine: Emphasis on peace, concord, and maintaining stability Tendency to avoid struggle and suppress their private dreams.

Type One: Driven through the usage of a choice for perfection, correctness, and development May battle with a critical inner voice.

2. Heart Centre (Feeling Centre) The Heart Centre consists of sorts Two, Three, and Four. People on this centre are more attuned to their feelings and frequently rely on their emotions to make picks and apprehend their reviews. They fee relationships and their self confidence is frequently tied to how they are perceived with the useful resource of others.

Type Two: Driven via a need to be helpful, loved, and valued. Can be generous however may also conflict with boundaries.

Type Three: Strives for success, recognition, and efficiency. May have issue connecting with actual feelings because of a focal point on photo.

Type Four: Focus on individuality, feelings, and location of knowledge. May enjoy excessive emotions and conflict with feelings of inadequacy.

three. Head Centre (Thinking Centre) The Head Centre encompasses kinds Five, Six, and Seven. Individuals on this centre rely closely on their mind, evaluation, and intellectual statistics of the arena. They frequently grapple with anxiety and uncertainty.

Type Five: Driven through a need for records, facts, and privacy. Can be withdrawn and may struggle with social interactions.

Type Six: Concerned with protection, loyalty, and making plans Tends to oscillate amongst searching out steering and doubting one.

Type Seven: Focus on variety, spontaneity, and retaining off ache Might battle with commitment and going through horrible emotions.

Understanding those centres of intelligence can provide insights into why positive kinds behave the way they do, how they way facts, and the way they relate to others. It's essential to be aware that at the same time as sorts inside the same centre share common inclinations, anyone is specific and advocated through the use of different factors beyond their Enneagram kind. Exploring those centres can assist beautify communique, solve conflicts, and foster better relationships via spotting and appreciating unique methods of perceiving and responding to the arena. An important issue of Enneagram compatibility is the popularity that every type has strengths and demanding situations. Partnerships amongst sorts can flourish whilst people understand and recognize every other's particular characteristics. For example, the analytical nature of a Type 5 can complement the keenness of a Type 7, fostering a balanced and insightful relationship.

Understanding Wings

The Enneagram, frequently notion of as a sincere diagram boxing us into one in every of 9 person categories, has more to offer than first meets the eye. It presents a deeper layer, regularly omitted but critical—wings. Imagine those wings due to the reality the substances that increase a easy daal to an fragrant daal makhani. The wings sit down beside your maximum critical Enneagram kind, bringing in complexities and nuances that make every personality uniquely captivating, truly as each person in our severa state is.

A commonplace belief indicates that a person is mainly described through manner in their middle Enneagram type. While available, this overlooks the complexity that every human brings to the table. Consider a Type Nine individual, commonly called the Peacemaker. Now, adjoining to this Type Nine are wings—Eight and One. These wings add layers to the Peacemaker's center tendencies. It's as even though the vital nature of the Type Nine is a certain canvas, and the wings—each Eight or One—provide the brushstrokes that make it a masterpiece. Pioneers like Don Richard Riso and Russ Hudson have thrown slight at the significance of wings within the Enneagram. Riso perspectives those wings as factors that improve your center identity, much like how various sun shades add depth to a painting.

Hudson draws a similar analogy, comparing wings to solar sun shades of colour that make the entire photo greater colourful. Just as a rainbow is incomplete without the concord of its shades, an character's Enneagram kind lacks fullness with out considering the wings.

An interesting trouble of wings is the speak on their amount. While it's easy that every kind has adjoining wings, they don't usually have an effect on the middle type equally. Most human beings are swayed more by manner of 1 wing than the alternative. For example, in case you are a Type Two, usually referred to as the Helper, you could lean closer to both a Three-wing, referred to as the Achiever, or a One-wing, called the Reformer. The lesser wing isn't absent; it actually doesn't assert itself as strongly because the dominant one. Some professionals additionally word that as people age or expand psychologically, the much much less dominant wing begins offevolved offevolved to come to be extra influential.

Whether this takes place universally is a subject that beckons further test. Identifying your center Enneagram type is simply the start line. Tools much like the Riso-Hudson Enneagram Type Indicator exist that will help you pinpoint not genuinely your center kind but your capability wings. It's essential to bear in mind that those machine have obstacles; they can not encapsulate the intricacy of human character. Real perception comes from reading significantly approximately your middle kind and searching how your wings show up in terrific life conditions.

Why hassle with wings in any respect? Understanding your wing can offer pathways to private growth. This understanding can help you become aware of your motivations and fears. It moreover has broader implications for interpersonal relationships. Knowing your wings can mild up why you join effects with a few human beings and discover it hard with others.

Enneagram isn't just a static circle however a dynamic version. Wings upload a layer of richness to the number one sorts. They help us apprehend that we are greater than honestly a unique considerable variety; we are a mix of various factors that together shape our complex personalities. Just much like the layers of data in an historical city, the ones layers make us compelling, difficult, and profoundly human

Chapter 12: Enneagram And Inter-Relationships

Arrows and the Path of Integration

Arrows in the Enneagram system are akin to road signs and symptoms and symptoms in our journey of self-discovery. They manual us to certain paths below diverse instances, directing us both closer to increase or displaying us wherein we would falter under stress. While the center Enneagram kind is your own home base, those arrows suggest routes towards differing types that have an effect in your behaviour and personality in a profound way. Understanding the mechanism of those arrows offers a greater nuanced photo of how we feature and adapt in unique lifestyles eventualities.

Consider a Type 1, normally referred to as 'The Perfectionist'. This individual has the tendency to conform with the aid of adopting traits of a Type 7, who is 'The Enthusiast'. Under excessive superb conditions, our Type 1 might discover themselves exploring new pastimes and embracing spontaneity, breaking free from the shackles of hysteria. Conversely, even as confronted with disturbing conditions or strain, the identical man or woman can also gravitate inside the route of traits of a Type four, labelled 'The Individualist', wherein their behaviour may also additionally need to become extra emotionally charged and focused inwardly.

To completely draw close this dynamic, it's essential to check the Enneagram diagram itself. Arrows be part of your center kind to those other sorts, forming nearly a triangular connection. One arrow leads you closer to a type that well-known your inherent pressure responses, and the alternative one courses you to a type representing your most beneficial course for private increase. In essence, those arrows characteristic suggestions for know-how not absolutely who you're, however furthermore how you could extend or how you may react while you're not at your wonderful. These arrows, therefore, don't simply illustrate your tendencies; they narrate the unfolding story of your personal evolution.

Arrows act as a balancing act

Arrows introduce a balancing act amongst your middle type, stress kind, and increase type. While your middle kind remains your basis, statistics your reactions below stress and your functionality for growth gives a whole view of your Enneagram journey. It's like navigating thru existence with an adaptable compass that guides you via numerous situations. Over the direction of its development, there has been a nuanced evolution in the interpretation of those lines and arrows. Initially, a simplified mind-set emerged, suggesting a dichotomy among "real" and "awful" arrows, much like increase and pressure actions. However, a more whole know-how has considering that emerged, highlighting the significance of embracing every commands of movement for holistic personal development.

At its inception, the Enneagram's arrows have been perceived as signs of development. Moving along the "particular" arrow have become believed to indicate boom, at the same time as traversing the "bad" arrow represented disintegration. This interpretation contributed to a view of integration as a right kingdom and disintegration as a problem to private improvement. Consequently, this attitude created a dichotomy that oversimplified the complex approaches that arise inside everyone's Enneagram adventure. But it's now understood that every arrow points offer valuable expansions for each persona type, fostering a balanced and properly-rounded man or woman. Instead of a linear development closer to boom and far from stress, the Enneagram recognizes the need for a holistic method that includes each instructions.

Arrows introduce a compelling dance of stability the diverse middle type, strain kind, and boom type. The middle type serves as the foundation, representing an individual's essential individual trends and dispositions. The pressure type captures the way an person responds beneath stress, at the identical time due to the fact the boom kind embodies the aspirational trends that one may want to mix into their individual. This interaction creates a rich tapestry of trends and behaviours that mirror the complexity of human nature.

Navigating the Enneagram journey is much like wielding an adaptable compass. The compass doesn't simply aspect in a single direction; it dynamically adjusts to numerous landscapes, guiding one through top notch terrains. Similarly, the Enneagram's arrows provide a multifaceted manual thru lifestyles's various situations, permitting humans to attract upon both growth and pressure components as they come across annoying conditions and opportunities.

Chapter 13: Embracing Redemption

The Journey of Redeemed and Unredeemed Enneagram Types

In the Enneagram, the idea of redemption is a watch constant-opener. It makes us apprehend that human personality is not set in stone, that it can evolve. The concept is simple: human beings can trade, not only a little, but in strategies that rely. So, permit's communicate approximately this concept of 'redemption' with none excessive-sounding terms or convoluted theories.

When we speak over with an 'unredeemed' kind inside the context of the Enneagram, what we suggest is a persona however stuck up in its very non-public barriers. These are developments, behaviours, or attitudes that hold us lower again in some manner. It can be an immoderate need for approval from others, or a bent to be overly essential, or a addiction of procrastinating important duties. Whatever form it takes, the 'unredeemed' component is a few aspect that doesn't assist us live our lives to the fullest. It limits our increase, maintains us caught in acquainted however unhelpful styles, and every now and then even causes us troubles in our relationships and careers.

So, what takes vicinity while an 'unredeemed' trait becomes 'redeemed'? First of all, it doesn't suggest the trait disappears or will become its unique contrary. Rather, it evolves into a shape that serves us higher. For instance, someone who's overly vital could in all likelihood come to be discerning as an alternative. They would despite the fact that be conscious records others may also moreover miss, however in region of simply pointing out what's wrong, they may moreover see solutions and opportunities for development.

The journey from unredeemed to redeemed is a piece like cleansing a cluttered room. At first, you could sense crushed with the aid of the mess. But as you sort via it piece with the aid of using piece, finding out what to maintain, what to throw away, and what to arrange, the room starts offevolved offevolved to address a brand new shape. In a similar manner, the method of redeeming one's tendencies involves some sincere self-exam. It asks us to have a have a look at components of ourselves we would opt to ignore or keep away from, to preserve them as lots as the slight and word them for what they will be. It's pleasant thru doing this that we're able to start to recognize how those trends may be converted into a few trouble greater useful, more fantastic.

And how does one embark on this journey of redemption? First, by means of the usage of manner of turning into privy to one's unredeemed trends. This can occur in loads of processes: through self-mirrored image, thru remarks from others, or maybe via a catastrophe that makes you recognize some thing wants to alternate. Once you're privy to what needs redeeming, the subsequent step is to understand it deeply. This technique asking questions like: Why do I behave this way? What fears or dreams are the use of this trait? What could occur if I acted in some other way?

Once you have a first-rate hold close of the 'why', the route to 'how' becomes clearer. Often, the adventure entails changing antique, unhelpful behaviours with new, greater healthy ones. This isn't clean and takes time, but it's absolutely possible. Tools like mindfulness, cognitive behavioural techniques, or even easy practices like journaling can be genuinely beneficial right here. The cause is to make the redeemed trait a modern day dependancy, so deeply ingrained that it becomes a natural a part of who you are.

So, why hassle with all this? The answer is straightforward: redeeming your trends ends in a fuller, happier life. It permits you to interact with the arena in a more authentic way, to construct higher relationships, and to discover more pride for your paintings. It allows you increase as someone. And that's some component everybody want, isn't it? The idea of redemption within the Enneagram offers us a framework to decorate and increase. It teaches us that the additives of our character that hold us again aren't immutable. They may be understood, transformed, or maybe become strengths. This is a powerful message, one that opens up new opportunities for human increase and happiness. It's a message well well worth taking to coronary coronary heart.

The Redemption Journey: A Path to Wholeness

The adventure in the direction of redemption in the Enneagram framework is an exploration honestly well worth undertaking. It begins offevolved, as maximum journeys do, with acknowledgment. To keep away from addressing one's unredeemed tendencies is to empower them further, permitting them to perform from the unconscious corners of 1's personality. After acknowledgment, which serves as the doorway gate to this quest, we come face to face with the concept of self-interest. It's not surely about introspection but approximately actively dissecting your mind, behaviours, and emotions to discover what fuels them. For a Type 1, who is manifestly willing in the route of perfectionism and an acute enjoy of right and incorrect, it's about probing deeper to find out the underlying want for order and control. Do they stem from a youth memory or an innate preference for social approval? It's approximately connecting the dots to shape a coherent knowledge of oneself.

Now that you realize why your unredeemed trends exist, what's subsequent? The direction of redemption gives no shortcuts; as an alternative, it needs rigorous practices, first-rate-tuned to man or woman desires. Consider cognitive-behavioural remedy, a way that's been immensely useful in coping with difficult idea styles. A Type eight, who might probable showcase dominating tendencies, can benefit from this shape of treatment to apprehend how they are able to wield their innate control capabilities without overshadowing others. But once in a while, our emotional barriers are so deeply entrenched that they seem as bodily blockages in the frame. This is wherein practices like yoga can be useful. For example, a Type 9, diagnosed for their peace-loving demeanour, would in all likelihood suppress their emotions to keep away from conflicts, leading to physical strain. Yoga, in such times, permits in liberating this suppressed emotional anxiety.

Therapy is definitely one component of the coin; the other is non-stop monitoring and evaluation. An effective device for this is journaling. Keeping a every day record not extremely good offers a vicinity to write emotions and research however also serves as a dependable approach to have a observe changes, patterns, and changes. Regular magazine entries assist in actively monitoring the path of one's journey toward redemption. Here, a Type three, who is probably overly targeted on accomplishments, can hint another time their dispositions to are searching for validation from outside achievements and reconsider their values and desires.

While the characteristic of experts within the realm of the Enneagram can't be overstated, it’s equally important to have interaction in relationships that foster growth. Meaningful relationships act as mirrors reflecting each the quality and horrible, due to this assisting in self-assessment. A Type 5, who frequently detaches from emotional realities, can advantage immensely from such relationships, which challenge them to be extra gift and related. These relationships emerge as catalysts for alternate, pushing you from your consolation zones, thinking your actions, and compelling you to develop.

Chapter 14: The Enneagram System

The Enneagram is attributed to historical cultural origins, and come to be first added to the contemporary global with the beneficial resource of Russian-Armenian trainer George Gurdjieff, who mounted it as a intellectual development device. It come to be later adapted as a character typing tool by using the usage of Bolivian trainer Oscar Ichazo, after which integrated with ideas of Western psychology with the useful resource of the usage of Chilean psychiatrist Claudio Naranjo. Further tendencies at the Enneagram tool had been later made through tremendous instructors which include Russ Hudson, Don Richard Riso, and A.H. Almaas.

The Enneagram of Personality is a gadget of 9 one of a kind persona kinds numbered One to Nine. The nine sorts constitute precise techniques an individual's man or woman constellates round really one in all 3 number one bad feelings: anger, fear, and grief. Accordingly, the 9 types are assembled into three fundamental groups, also known as 'Triads':

The Anger Triad (Types Eight, Nine, and One)

The Grief Triad (Types Two, Three, and Four)

The Fear Triad (Types Five, Six, and Seven)

In regard to the names of these Triads, numerous factors should be stated:

The three Triads are regularly known as the Gut Triad (Anger), the Heart Triad (Grief), and the Head Triad (Fear). In this e-book, the Triads are named after their underlying primary emotions (anger, fear, and grief) for the reason that talk will especially attention on those emotions.

'Anger' proper right here is used synonymously with rage, despite the fact that the precise definitions for those terms might also moreover moreover range from vicinity to area among not unusual usage.

Often, the phrase 'Shame' is used in region of 'Grief' to designate the underlying emotion of

Types Two, Three, and Four. While each grief and shame suggest a distressed united states of america of the united states of emotional fall apart, 'Grief' is more suitable whilst you recall that it is a primary emotion. Shame is a secondary emotion. This is in settlement with Enneagram authors collectively with Peter O'Hanrahan.

The Grief Triad is also often known as the Image Triad because of the tendency to over-hassle with self-photograph in Grief Types.

During early young people, a tough enjoy might be predominantly felt as a model of either anger, fear, or grief, depending on the character's emotional temperament or character. These versions shape the idea of the nine Enneagram Types. All 9 kind patterns exist indoors every humans, but one pattern might be dominant, ensuing in the dominant Enneagram Type.

The following is a brief description of the nine kinds regarding their precise emotional sample and traditional traits. These developments are given as they may be defined in the Enneagram Institute.

The Anger Triad

Type Eights (The Challenger) cope with their anger by means of taking an oppositional stance within the course of others and the sector. They have a propensity to be self-assured, decisive, willful, and confrontational.

Type Nines (The Peacemaker) deny their anger, and as a end result, they're typically ignorant of it and typically avoid conflict. They will be inclined to be receptive, reassuring, complacent, and resigned.

Type Ones (The Reformer) cope with their anger through the usage of looking to control and suppress it, ensuing in a crucial thoughts-set in the direction of themselves and others. They have a propensity to be principled, useful, self-managed, and perfectionistic.

The Grief Triad

Type Twos (The Helper) cope with their grief thru manner of trying to benefit love from others and being visible as beneficial and worrying. They have a tendency to be generous, demonstrative, people-relevant, and possessive.

Type Threes (The Achiever) cope with their grief via denying it and try to be visible as valuable and a hit within the eyes of others. They tend to be adaptable, excelling, driven, and photograph-aware.

Type Fours (The Individualist) deal with their grief with the aid of manner of turning into preoccupied with their enjoy of identification and distinctiveness. They have a tendency to be expressive, dramatic, self-absorbed, and temperamental.

The Fear Triad

Type Fives (The Investigator) fear being beaten and now not capable of address the outer international. They cope with this worry thru taking flight into their inner, mental worldwide. They have a tendency to be perceptive, innovative, secretive, and remoted.

Type Sixes (The Loyalist) address their worry with the useful aid of finding safety from one in all a type resources which includes relationships, alliances, or perception structures. They have a tendency to be appealing, accountable, stressful, and suspicious.

Type Sevens (The Enthusiast) worry their internal worldwide and try and keep away from feelings of pain and loss. They deal with this fear with the aid of the usage of retaining their minds distracted and appealing in stimulating sports activities activities inside the outer international. They tend to be spontaneous, flexible, acquisitive, and scattered.

Types Nine, Three, and Six are known as middle kinds, representing the essential and undifferentiated styles of their respective bad feelings. Type Nine embodies undifferentiated anger, Type Three embodies undifferentiated grief, and Type Six embodies undifferentiated worry. The very last six sorts are known as the Hexad Types, representing specialized variations of their respective middle types. Types Eight and One are specialised versions of Type Nine, Types Two and Four are specialised versions of Type Three, and Types Five and Seven are specialized variations of Type Six.

The Enneagram Symbol

The Enneagram is portrayed as a circle in which every of the 9 sorts is located at identical distances along the outside (Figure 1.1). Inside the circle are several connecting lines showing how the 9 types are associated with each one-of-a-kind. More about those relationships may be given within the next segment.

The Enneagram as a Spectrum

Each Enneagram Type may be understood as a hybrid among its adjoining types on the

Enneagram circle. For example, Type Two can be taken into consideration as a hybrid of Types One and Three. As such, the Enneagram can be likened to a colour spectrum, wherein every kind acts like a band of colour.

The Wings

No character is a natural man or woman kind; every Enneagram Type has a dishonest to tackle a secondary feature from one of the adjacent sorts at the circle. This secondary function is known as the wing, which may be seen as the second factor of the personality, an extension of the dominant type. Where each of the nine Enneagram Types is form of a coloration on a spectrum, the wings can give a kind greater tones. For example, a Type Seven can address secondary tendencies of Type Eight and, therefore, be referred to as a Seven wing Eight, or it could address secondary dispositions from Type Six and, consequently, be referred to as a Seven wing Six.

The Lines of Stress and Growth

The Enneagram picture (Figure 1.1) suggests how the 9 sorts are related and related. There are numerous connecting traces inside the circle. Each Enneagram Type is set up to 2 other kinds through those inner strains. The traces constitute how every type responds and behaves beneath specific conditions. One line, the Direction of Growth, shows how a kind behaves at the same time as they'll be steady, thriving and developing. The different line, the Direction of Stress, represents how a type behaves beneath strain or loss of control.

For example, Type Five is attached to Type Seven (thru the Direction of Stress) and Type Eight (via the Direction of Growth). Under annoying situations, a Type Five will behave further to an risky version of Type Seven, becoming distracted and mentally scattered. However, while a Type Five feels solid and secure, they may normally generally tend to act similarly to a healthy version of Type Eight, displaying energy and decisiveness.

The route of each type's Line of Stress and Line of Growth are examined inside the following desk:

The Three Instinctual Drives

The Enneagram device similarly identifies three Instinctual Drives (also called Instincts). These are organic tactics that encourage people to interact in positive behaviors, with a purpose to promote their survival and the survival in their species. The Instincts are crucial to our functioning as herbal organisms and, as such, have a massive have an impact on on our personalities.

The 3 Instinctual Drives are:

The Self-Preservation Instinct: concerned with survival, properly-being, and protection.

The Sexual Instinct: worried with appeal, courtship display, and sexual opposition.

The Social Instinct: worried with social connections, relatedness, and intimacy.

Every person has (in addition to the 9 type styles) all the Instinctual Drives running internal them. However, for every person, one of the Instincts is extra prioritized than the others. This is known as the dominant Instinct and could get maintain of the most attention and hobby. The dominant Instinct, as a result, has a stronger affect at the character than the alternative Instincts, and could drastically shape an man or woman's attitudes and values. Everything in the individual will gravitate around being capable of meet the wishes of the dominant Instinct. As such, everybody might also moreover have a dominant Instinctual Drive and a dominant Enneagram Type pattern.

A character with a dominant Self-Preservation Instinct is known as a Self-Preservation Type and is mainly involved with subjects of survival, well-being, and manner of lifestyles. A person with a dominant Sexual Instinct is called a Sexual Type, and is commonly concerned with generating a enjoy of appeal and chemistry in their activities and interplay with others. A individual with a dominant Social Instinct is called a Social Type and is inside the predominant concerned with their social relationships.

Each character additionally has a 2nd and a 3rd Instinctual Drive. The 2nd Instinct plays a secondary function and abilties as a assist to the dominant Instinct. The Third Instinct is the least superior of the 3 and is also called the Blindspot. The wishes of the Blindspot aren't given loads hobby and are frequently ignored.

The order of affiliation by means of the use of manner of which the 3 Instincts' needs are prioritized in someone is called the "Instinctual Stack." The Instincts can be considered to be stacked over every awesome constant with which one is dominant, 2d, and 1/three (Figure 1.2), with the dominant Instinct on top, the second inside the middle, and the 0.33 at the bottom.

A man or woman's Instinctual Stack is referred to as according to the number one Instincts. For instance, a person with a dominant Social Instinct, a 2nd Sexual Instinct, and a third Self-Preservation Instinct is probably referred to as a Social Sexual Type.

Further, the dominant Enneagram Type sample influences how the dominant Instinct is expressed. Therefore, the persona will extra accurately be described through way of way of mixing the Enneagram Type with the dominant Instinctual Drive. There are 27 viable combos of Enneagram Types and Instinctual Drives, identified collectively because the Instinctual Variants. For instance, a Type Four whose dominant Instinct is Social is stated to be a Social Four. A Type Nine whose dominant Instinct is Self-Preservation is said to be a Self-Preservation Nine, and so forth.

The following are short descriptions of the 3 Instincts and the manner they display up in a person who has them as their dominant Instinct:

The Self-Preservation Instinct

The Self-Preservation Instinct is the force for survival and well-being. It is concerned with topics of health, comfort, meals, safe haven, routine, and fabric protection. People whose dominant Instinct is Self-Preservation have a tendency to popularity on assembly the ones needs; they are regularly disciplined, almost orientated, and function the capacity to set dreams and satisfy them.

The Sexual Instinct

The Sexual Instinct arises from the primal urge to reproduce and make certain one's genetic cloth may want to make it into the following generation. It is extra than truly a force for copy; it also includes the act of courtship show and attracting big others. People with a dominant Sexual Instinct are often preoccupied with chasing the sensation of ‘chemistry’ and locating compatibility with some other man or woman. This can consist of a sexual accomplice, lover, or friend. They constantly are trying to find excessive and stimulating relationships, pastimes, and sports, and experience becoming definitely immersed and merged with them. This revel in of merging is not to be burdened with social intimacy, it certainly is a problem of the Social Instinct.

The Social Instinct

The Social Instinct is the electricity for social relatedness and intimacy. People with a dominant Social Instinct want to revel in a enjoy of belonging and try to hook up with others. They are often well-attuned to other people. They can also moreover actively try and form new own family participants and feature a keen eye for social hierarchies, the use of this to raise their function and social status. The Social Instinct can encourage someone to behave altruistically, defensive and preserving organizations for the greater particular of each person involved.

Chapter 15: The Theory Of Evolution

The concept of evolution is a systematic framework that explains how species evolve and adapt through the years. It end up first proposed via Charles Darwin inside the mid-19th century and has considering become one of the cornerstone ideas in biology. According to this concept, all lifestyles on Earth shares a not unusual ancestor and has been evolving for billions of years, resulting in the terrific form of life we see nowadays.

Evolution is pushed via key mechanisms: genetic mutations and herbal selection. Genetic mutations are random adjustments that arise within the DNA of an individual organism. Most mutations are independent or harmful, but sometimes, they may be useful. Beneficial mutations offer an advantage to the man or woman in its surroundings, inclusive of better camouflage or more potent resistance to diseases. These wonderful developments increase the individual's chances of survival and replica, consequently growing the probability of passing on those beneficial inclinations to future generations. Conversely, individuals with much less favorable tendencies are a whole lot much less in all likelihood to stay on and reproduce, resulting in a decreased incidence of these inclinations within the next technology. Over time, beneficial dispositions turn out to be more common within the population, at the identical time as terrible traits turn out to be less acquainted. This manner, in which some trends are desired over others, is known as herbal preference.

In this way, genetic mutation and natural choice paintings collectively to energy the procedure of evolution, fundamental to the sluggish alternate and variation of species to their environments Over lots and plenty of years, the buildup of small modifications can cause exquisite adjustments, resulting in the emergence of recent species.

Evolution has original the extraordinary kind of existence on our planet, from bacteria to people. Through endless generations, evolution has given upward push to numerous species that have tailored to their environments in extremely good and precise techniques. Amidst this journey, all vertebrate animal schooling emerged, which includes fish, amphibians, reptiles, birds, and mammals, every with their non-public super tendencies and evolutionary advantages.

Fish have been maximum of the earliest vertebrates to emerge, round 530 million years inside the beyond. They tailored to their aquatic habitats by using way of the usage of evolving streamlined our bodies, gills for extracting oxygen from the water, and fins for swimming. This enabled them to thrive in severa aquatic environments. Over time, a few fish ventured out of the water, gradually adapting to existence on land These creatures have end up the ancestors of amphibians, which incorporates frogs and salamanders. They possessed each lungs and gills, allowing them to breathe every in water and on land. They moreover evolved limbs to transport on land, regardless of the truth that they but depended on water for reproduction.

As the years passed, sure corporations of land-living amphibians advanced defensive scales and the capability to put their eggs in waterproof instances, decreasing their dependence on water. These diversifications introduced approximately the emergence of reptiles In due path, reptiles diversified into diverse lineages. One institution of reptiles tailored to existence within the air and advanced into the primary birds. Another institution of reptiles began to reveal mammalian traits, sooner or later giving rise to proper mammals.

Evidence for the concept of evolution is derived from numerous belongings, which includes fossil records, comparative anatomy, embryology, and molecular genetics. Fossils provide a chronological document of past life forms, displaying the sluggish changes in species over the years. Comparative anatomy permits scientists to examine similarities and variations the diverse frame systems of numerous species. Embryology examines the similarities in the early degrees of development among terrific species. Molecular genetics offers evidence of genetic similarities and versions among species.

The Hierarchy of the Brain

Before discussing how one-of-a-kind character patterns ought to probable emerge from the mind, it's far first vital to grow to be acquainted with the thoughts's neuroanatomical form. The mind includes numerous anatomical layers that can be divided in distinctive strategies. Functionally, the ones brain layers may be divided into the hindbrain, midbrain, limbic device, and cerebral cortex (Figure 1.Three). The hindbrain is the maximum primitive in terms of its abilities, carrying out some of the maximum fundamental strategies. The midbrain and limbic structures are accountable for skills of intermediate complexity. Finally, the cerebral cortex is wherein advanced cognitive tactics arise. Thus, the mind is prepared proper right into a hierarchical form, in which each layer performs more and more complicated abilties.

Hindbrain

The hindbrain is the amazing middle of the mind. It includes the cerebellum, reticular formation, and the decrease part of the mind stem. Evolutionarily speakme, the hindbrain includes the oldest and most primitive additives of the mind, having existed for masses of its evolutionary history. It is accountable for simple physical strategies critical for survival, at the facet of breathing, coronary coronary heart rate, blood pressure, digestion, coordination of motion, and balance.

Midbrain

The midbrain makes up the top a part of the mind stem. It includes systems which encompass the tectum, the cerebral peduncles, and the tegmentum It capabilities as a bridge, connecting the decrease and pinnacle factors of the thoughts, making it a relay station for the primary concerned machine. The midbrain is involved in functions relating to seen and auditory processing, alertness, emotional responses and manage of movement.

Limbic System

The limbic tool incorporates a collection of interconnected systems, consisting of the amygdala, hypothalamus, hippocampus, and components of the thalamus. It is likewise known as the proto-mammalian brain, because of its presence in mammals. The limbic device controls emotional responses, memory, hormone launch, hunger and thirst, sexual responses, and temperature law.

Cerebral Cortex

The cerebral cortex is the outermost layer of the mind and consists of folds referred to as gyri. The biggest element is the neocortex, composed of the frontal, parietal, occipital, and temporal lobes. The cerebral cortex is domestic to the very best-diploma cognitive processing in the mind. It contains out the abilties of language, reminiscence, precis notion and reasoning, complicated choice-making, pattern recognition, processing sensory facts, and speech.

The Neuroscience of Emotion

Research into the technology of emotion has made big improvement in present day years, in massive element manner to advances in technological strategies along facet mind imaging. These advances have enabled researchers to map neural pathways and feature a have a look at the techniques that underlie emotional evaluations. As such, they are able to create practical models of the way feelings feature within the thoughts.

Based on discoveries made thru neural mapping of the mind, number one emotional responses were determined to emerge from the midbrain and limbic system (Panksepp &

Biven, 2012). These number one emotional responses are then in addition modulated and changed with the aid of manner of manner of higher areas in the neocortex. The neocortex acts as a manipulate middle, permitting us to mirror and contemplate on our feelings and modify how we manipulate and explicit them. For example, whilst an individual is indignant, the uncooked emotion of rage emerges from the midbrain and limbic device however is then modulated with the useful useful resource of the neocortex to be expressed in approaches which may be pretty ideal to the surrounding network. Much of this processing is determined via societal norms and expectancies that we've found out. So in desire to flying into a rage, we can manipulate our anger and keep away from worsening the situation. As such, the neocortex regulates and modifies emotional responses, however isn't always accountable for growing them.

Furthermore, primary emotional responses are inborn and "hardwired" into the midbrain and limbic device, whilst the neocortex is basically a easy slate while an individual is born. The capabilities and talents of the neocortex are determined out and advanced as we have interaction and have interaction with the environment.

All mammals percentage a similar set of number one emotional strategies springing up from the subcortical networks in the midbrain and limbic tool. However, the neocortex will vary pretty in characteristic and length from species to species, being especially huge and well-advanced in people.

Animals experience emotions; they worry damage, are looking for comfort, and experience play Emotional responses which includes worry and rage are commonplace at some point of the animal state and can be located in mammals, birds, reptiles, and fish. (Panksepp & Biven, 2012; Davis & Panksepp, 2018)

This makes experience thinking about the evolutionary importance of emotions. Emotions are powerful for survival because of the truth they will be inner sensors that speedy permit an animal to react to a scenario within the external surroundings, regularly at the same time as not having preceding learning. For example, worry is an emotional reaction which could assist an animal escape from a predator, therefore saving its life. Affection is an emotion that makes an animal cope with its offspring; an act which allows propagates the species with the useful resource of increasing the possibilities of the offspring surviving. In evolutionary phrases, emotional responses are based totally on high excellent genetic traits which might be handed down from one generation to the subsequent those born without these trends is probably a good buy lots less possibly to live to tell the tale and reproduce.

The scientific have a have a look at of feelings within the mind is usefully finished thru animal research. This is because of the truth human emotional techniques are pretty complicated and intertwined with better cognitive strategies. Thus, animal research provides a much less complex manner of reading emotions. Primary emotional brain techniques characteristic in similar techniques in the direction of tremendous species, specially among mammals. Animals can feature beneficial fashions to base and test complex hypotheses that could assist decipher emotional hobby in the human brain. A pioneer of this kind of animal studies changed into neuroscientist Jaak Panksepp.

The Seven Primary-Process Emotional Systems

Jaak Panksepp come to be a leading determine inside the field of affective neuroscience, which studies how emotions upward thrust up in the mind. Through his neurobiological investigations in mammals, he charted seven primary emotional networks inside the midbrain and limbic system. These networks are genetically inborn and hardwired into the thoughts. In distinctive phrases, they may be instinctive and, consequently, do not need to be determined out. Panksepp referred to as those the number one-method emotional structures, figuring out FEAR, RAGE, GRIEF, SEEKING, LUST, CARE, and PLAY. Each reasons extraordinary affective testimonies and behaviors inside the animal. They are capitalized to distinguish them from the normal usage of those words.

These emotional systems emerged very early inside the direction of brain evolution, bobbing up from historical systems deep within the most primitive elements of the thoughts. They are commonplace to all mammals, which includes people, and the earliest of these systems can also also be studied in fish and reptiles.

Each number one-way emotional machine follows an ascending pathway that runs up from the midbrain to the limbic machine, and ultimately connects to better thoughts regions inside the neocortex. The PAG (periaqueductal grey) is an essential location within the midbrain this is concerned in all of these emotional structures. The PAG may be seen due to the fact the headquarters—the "Grand Central Station"—that those primary emotional systems run via. This is in comparison to the often incorrect belief that the amygdala is the headquarters of emotion within the mind. The amygdala participates greater in some emotional systems than others, and isn't always the most precious aspect.

FEAR, RAGE, GRIEF, SEEKING, LUST, CARE, and PLAY are considered to be emotional systems due to the truth they produce affective behavioral responses. These are consistent modes of reaction to the environment that help animals live to tell the story and consist of instinctual responses and raw, unmodified emotions.

Each of the primary emotional systems has each a excellent or awful valence; they may reason enchantment or aversion in response to a given scenario. FEAR, RAGE, and GRIEF are modes of negative reaction, generating the primary feelings of worry, rage, and grief. SEEKING, LUST, CARE, and PLAY are modes of extremely good reaction, producing the number one emotions of pleasure, sexual lust, affection, and satisfaction, respectively.

The following is a quick review of the seven number one-device emotional structures in the brain:

The FEAR System

The characteristic of the FEAR tool is to sign danger and orient the animal, honestly so it could avoid and get away the danger. It motives physiological modifications in the body, consisting of advanced coronary coronary heart rate and blood drift. It can motive awesome varieties of behaviors depending on the perceived hazard degree, mobilizing the animal to get away or inflicting it to freeze in its location. When the FEAR machine is activated, the animal can also want to have a terrible, stressful enjoy that urges it to interrupt out from the FEAR-inducing stimulus, and the associated physiological changes will useful resource it in doing in order short as viable. When the FEAR device is experimentally inspired in human beings, subjects record feelings of immoderate fearfulness and tension without a obvious cause.

The FEAR network runs through the PAG (periaqueductal grey), hypothalamus and amygdala.

The RAGE System

The RAGE device lets in an animal to guard itself and fight toward competitors. It is commonly activated at the same time as an animal has trouble in assembly its desires or even as it's miles limited or confined. When the RAGE reaction is evoked, animals will pass inside the path of the motive of their frustration and engage in competitive behaviors which consist of biting and scratching. Stimulation of the RAGE machine in humans reasons immoderate anger assaults.

This tool's neural network runs via the PAG, hypothalamus, and amygdala.

The GRIEF System

The GRIEF device is activated even as an person will become separated from their caregiver or cherished one, and is associated with feelings of distress, unhappiness, and loss. It can reason a younger animal to show off misery vocalizations (crying), with a view to be observed through their caregiver and make certain they're taken care of. If touch with the caregiver isn't always re-mounted, the younger animal will steadily stop crying and crumble right into a country much like despair. It is concept that human grief and sadness are due to the GRIEF tool.

The GRIEF device is positioned within the PAG, thalamus, and anterior cingulate gyrus.

The SEEKING System

The SEEKING tool motivates an animal to are searching for out resources crucial for survival. It is associated with exploratory, appetitive, and inquisitive behaviors that advantage character animals with the useful resource of supporting them find food, secure haven, and distinct useful property. It motivates them to engage and interact with their environment, and inspires emotions of satisfaction, anticipation, and hobby.

The SEEKING tool is likewise concerned in all the different emotional structures and plays a assisting characteristic in their functioning. For example, whilst coupled with the LUST or PLAY structures, it arouses a experience of cause and interest.

The thoughts areas associated with the SEEKING system are the PAG, hypothalamus, ventral tegmental region (VTA), nucleus accumbens, and medial forebrain bundle deal. When activated, the SEEKING tool reasons the discharge of the brain chemical dopamine.

Chapter 16: The Lust System

The LUST system motivates animals to discover appropriate buddies and reproduce. It involves particular feelings associated with sexual attraction and arousal. The LUST machine activates animals to engage in dating and mating behaviors, which variety widely counting on the species.

Traditionally, sexual lust is regularly no longer taken into consideration an emotion but a physical intuition. However, Panksepp and masses of others argue that it must be appeared as an emotion because it produces complex instinctual behaviors, which may be feature of emotions.

The LUST device is located in the PAG, hypothalamus, and amygdala. It is carefully tied to the hobby of intercourse hormones like testosterone.

The CARE System

The CARE gadget promotes nurturing and being concerned behaviors. It in particular takes expression in the mom-infant dating, wherein it allows to ensure that offspring are nicely taken care of, and all in their simple dreams are met. The CARE system is related to feelings of affection and may result in severa affectionate behaviors, which includes caressing and embracing. Besides its role in mothering, it can additionally promote other social bonds wherein nurturance is involved.

The CARE system is positioned within the PAG and hypothalamus. It is related to hormones which include oxytocin and prolactin.

The PLAY System

The PLAY gadget promotes best interactions and enjoyment with different people. It stimulates laughter and playfulness and is specially lively sooner or later of adolescence. It activates animals to have interaction in amusing bodily sports activities like chasing, poking, and wrestling. These sports activities assist the animal have a look at social rules and broaden social bonds. Behaviors related to the PLAY machine are located via the usage of a experience of immoderate social pleasure.

The PLAY device is positioned in the PAG and thalamus.

Interactions between the Primary-Process Emotional Systems

The seven number one emotional structures do now not function one after the other; they'll be interconnected and interact with each different. For instance, at the same time as a mother's CARE tool is activated, motivating she to nurture her offspring, the SEEKING gadget can also be concerned, prompting her to are looking for meals and steady haven in order that she will be able to accurately provide care. Another example is on the identical time as an animal, brought on thru the SEEKING gadget, tries to locate meals however critiques problems in doing so. Such a scenario will spark off the RAGE system, which synergizes with the SEEKING system and empowers the animal to exert extra attempt.

The Three Levels of Emotional Brain Processing

Affective neuroscience identifies 3 levels of emotional processing within the thoughts: primary, secondary, and tertiary. In addition to the primary-method emotional structures, there also are secondary and tertiary emotional strategies, which permit the thoughts to modulate, take a look at from, and reflect upon the number one emotions. Each of those strategies exists in terrific thoughts regions, and they create a hierarchy that runs anatomically, from the midbrain to the limbic gadget and up to the neocortex. As proven in Figure 1.Four, the primary-technique emotions exist at the extent of the midbrain and limbic gadget, the secondary approaches stand up in huge detail in the limbic gadget, and the tertiary strategies inside the neocortex.

The following is a quick description of these strategies:

Primary-Process Emotions

These are the primary-method emotional systems described above: FEAR, RAGE, GREIF, SEEKING, LUST, CARE, and PLAY. They are placed inside the midbrain and limbic system, and generate uncooked number one emotional influences. The number one-approach emotions are the most important degree of emotional processing, from which the secondary and tertiary techniques emerge. They can be visible due to the fact the "number one sun shades" of emotions.

The primary-system feelings do now not want to be determined; they're inborn and hardwired into the thoughts. For example, a little one will instinctively grow to be sad and worried at the same time as separated from a determine. This emotional reaction does no longer require any gaining knowledge of.

Secondary Processes

The formerly defined primary-process feelings feature platforms upon which people can have a look at from their testimonies, forming emotional memories and conduct. Our most effective reminiscences are frequently of things that made an emotional effect on us, on the side of a catastrophic occasion or the lack of a loved one. This primitive emotional shape of mastering is called secondary processing, and takes region inside the top part of the limbic machine.

As referred to, the primary feelings are inner signs that inspire an person to react to a state of affairs, both drawing near (first-rate feelings) or keeping off and resisting (terrible emotions). These number one emotions are, therefore, both fantastic or unsightly. In mental language, excellent exquisite emotions are expert as rewards, on the equal time as unsightly poor emotions are skilled as punishments. After repeatedly going via the ones profitable or punishing reviews, the individual will modify their behavior; this is how studying takes place.

As such, learning allows an individual to conform and better meet the needs in their environment. Each primary-system emotional device will feature a platform, upon which this model can rise up.

For example, while an animal is confronted with a volatile state of affairs, a primary-approach FEAR response might be generated; it's professional as an unpleasant have an impact on. The animal will then routinely avoid comparable conditions inside the future. This is a secondary-technique placed out version. In this situation, the professional FEAR acted as a "punishing have an impact on" that made the animal examine from its revel in. This computerized studying may additionally moreover need to keep the animal's life, due to the fact the learned avoidance response will decrease the chance of the animal setting itself in that unstable situation another time.

Another example of secondary-method learning: The SEEKING device motivates an animal to discover its environment for resources, together with meals and shelter. When an animal correctly famous those sources, it's far rewarded with comfort, nourishment, and delight When this takes region, the mind workplace work an affiliation some of the SEEKING behaviors and the rewards. This makes the animal have a examine the advantage of those behaviors, and the memory of the exciting rewards will activate it to perform greater SEEKING behaviors in the destiny.

Another word for the primitive analyzing that occurs at the secondary-approach degree is conditioning, which was first determined by way of the use of the use of Ivan Pavlov. Pavlov finished experiments with dogs; he may additionally sound a metronome whenever he fed them and found that, through the years, the dogs ought to begin to salivate at the mere sound of the metronome, even when no meals have become given to them. In this test, the dogs' brains related the sound of the metronome with meals. This is known as a found conditioned response.

Secondary-way gaining knowledge of is emotional in its nature, and is largely subconscious and automated. It is not the intentional, calculated form of mastering we use even as studying new facts, together with 5x9 equals 45. For instance, a rat will mechanically and unconsciously learn how to worry the sound of a bell on a cat's collar; it will no longer consciously reason that the sound of the bell way danger. Similarly, most people who have dramatic lifestyles-converting reminiscences will have any choice in remembering the ones conditions; their brains will advantage this automatically.

Tertiary Processes

At the highest degree of the thoughts, a large variety of highbrow tactics are achieved. These are known as tertiary strategies and are based mostly on further adjustments of the number one and secondary techniques. They encompass making plans, preference-making, ruminations, and emotional reflections. The tertiary strategies stand up especially within the mind's neocortex, which dramatically differs in period, enterprise, and complexity throughout extraordinary species. The quit stop end result is that simply one in all a kind animals variety in their degree of intelligence and cognitive capabilities.

Tertiary methods permit people to assume abstractly, believe and create new mind, and synthesize requirements. They facilitate the contemplation of oneself and one's vicinity within the international, considering the beyond and future and numerous schooling discovered through lifestyles reviews. These abilities expand through the years and are refined with adulthood.

Tertiary techniques adjust secondary and number one techniques, refining the emotional responses that rise up from lower regions of the brain. Tertiary techniques can modulate the intensity, expression, and duration of emotional states, producing a extra state-of-the-art emotional reaction. However, they do no longer generate feelings themselves. To quote Panksepp: "Our better (neocortical) intellectual features can create paintings and insanity out of our feelings, but they can't generate feelings on their very very own." (Panksepp & Biven, 2012, p.Eighty one)

Tertiary strategies may be regarded as advanced processes to assist animals deal with their environment and meet their desires. However, reading tertiary tactics in animals is hard, as they cannot document their thoughts and reports.

The Nested Brain Hierarchy

The Nested Brain Hierarchy is a model that describes how the 3 techniques in the brain (primary, secondary and tertiary) are related to every exclusive. The primary-way emotions are the inspiration upon which the secondary techniques may be mounted, and the secondary techniques guide the formation of the tertiary techniques. As such, the primary-technique emotions are embedded (nested) and re-represented in secondary strategies, which can be, in turn, embedded within tertiary processes.

Thus, the number one-way emotions effect the conditioned studying that takes area on the secondary-method diploma, and the secondary methods manual the formation of higher cognitive capacities at the tertiary-device level. These are referred to as 'backside-up' impacts. At the equal time, tertiary techniques have an impact on secondary strategies via cognitive regulation, and secondary techniques manipulate primary techniques. These are known as 'top-down' impacts. The quit end result is a -way circular causation in the thoughts, in which the bottom-up and pinnacle-down manage mechanisms act in contrary commands. These mechanisms make the thoughts a very included unit, with all its approaches functioning in a cautiously coordinated and orchestrated manner.

In the early degrees of teenagers, bottom-up affects on studying, memory, and cognitive improvement are most energetic. However, later at some stage in formative years and maturity, the brain develops the functionality for top-down controls thru pretty a few tertiary techniques.

Figure 1.Five illustrates the Nested Brain Hierarchy. The primary, secondary, and tertiary techniques are interlinked and effect each different. The crimson square represents the number one-method emotions and is present on all three stages. The secondary strategies are hooked up as a green circle, integrating the primary-method feelings. The higher-degree abilities, shown as a large blue square, combine every the number one and secondary techniques.